AN INTRODUCTION TO STOICISM

PRACTICAL STOIC WISDOM TO CONQUER LIFE'S
GREATEST CHALLENGES

DAMIAN ALEXANDER

© **Copyright 2020 by JPPD Publishing International LLC - All rights reserved.**

The content contained within this book may not be reproduced, duplicated or transmitted without direct written permission from the author or the publisher.

Under no circumstances will any blame or legal responsibility be held against the publisher, or author, for any damages, reparation, or monetary loss due to the information contained within this book, either directly or indirectly.

Legal Notice:

This book is copyright protected. It is only for personal use. You cannot amend, distribute, sell, use, quote or paraphrase any part, or the content within this book, without the consent of the author or publisher.

Disclaimer Notice:

Please note the information contained within this document is for educational and entertainment purposes only. All effort has been executed to present accurate, up to date, reliable, complete information. No warranties of any kind are declared or implied. Readers acknowledge that the author is not engaged in the rendering of legal, financial, medical or professional advice. The content within this book has been derived from various sources. Please consult a licensed professional before attempting any techniques outlined in this book. By reading this document, the reader agrees that under no circumstances is the author responsible for any losses, direct or indirect, that are incurred as a result of the use of the information contained within this document, including, but not limited to, errors, omissions, or inaccuracies.

CONTENTS

Introduction	xv
I. What the Heck is Stoicism?	1
II. Stoicism Key Principles	29
III. The Ruler and The Subject	51
IV. The Stoic Practices	61
V. When Things Get Tough	85
VI. Timeless Wisdom	107
The 'Stoicism Classics' - Ultimate Bundle	135
Afterword	137
One Last Thing	139
References	141

The 'Stoicism Classics' collection includes:

1. The Meditations by Marcus Aurelius
2. The Discourses by Epictetus
3. Letters from a Stoic by Seneca

To get them for free, visit the following link:

www.unrivaledmind.com/classics

INTRODUCTION

"Today I escaped anxiety. Or no, I discarded it, because it was within me, in my own perceptions – not outside."

— *MARCUS AURELIUS*

Imagine a simple scenario most of us have faced – you're being blamed for a mistake at work, which a colleague did and attributed to you. Your manager is unmoving – you will have to face the repercussions.

Do you:

1. Lose sleep due to the unfairness of the situation
2. Become completely fixated to convince your boss you're not the one to blame
3. Start thinking of retaliation strategies
4. Assess the situation with a clear head, provide evidence, state your truth and move on

The last approach is the most difficult one to master and the one that would yield the best results. It's an approach based on millennia of philosophical wisdom about fate, our strengths, our weaknesses and the way in which we face life's challenges.

So, you want to know more about what Stoicism has to offer. Chances are you have a lot of questions about what this ancient philosophy is all about, and how it can benefit you; maybe you aren't sure where to start. Stoicism is going through a rebirth in the modern age, precisely because it is relevant to our everyday lives.

This book intends to guide a new Stoic seeking the path towards a fulfilling life. As a 53-year-old Stoic myself, I have greatly improved my life since I started this journey, and that is why I want to share it with you.

Before diving in into Stoicism, keep in mind that this isn't a religion, and I am not selling you salvation or anything of that kind. Stoicism is a great life philosophy where reason and wisdom rule above all.

In this book, you will learn about what it means to be a Stoic. You will discover the history of the philosophy and also absorb some of the wisdom that was left for us by famous philosophers from Ancient Greece and the Roman Empire. You will learn how to overcome the many obstacles that life throws at you and how to handle difficult situations.

I'm also going to dispel the many misconceptions about Stoicism. You will learn the principles and concepts behind living a life in which you have full control over yourself and your emotions. However, that doesn't mean that you will stop feeling. Being a Stoic is not about eradicating your emotions.

Stoicism puts you in the driver's seat. It gives you control of the one thing you can really conquer – your mind and your own responses to the world. The keys to a stronger mind, excellence of character, and a life-well-lived are hidden inside the pages of this book.

Life is too short to be consumed by regrets from the past or worries about the future. So, open your mind to the wisdom of the ancients, and let's discuss how such an old philosophy can improve your life.

I. WHAT THE HECK IS STOICISM?

Stoicism is one of the Hellenistic schools of philosophy. It was founded in Athens during the late third century BC by Zeno of Citium. The central doctrine of Stoicism is to "live in accordance with nature". For the Stoics, virtue is the only true good, and the path to happiness.

We need to rely only on ourselves and our actions as we cannot control any external events; we can only respond to them. Stoicism teaches us self-control, which will help us overcome our destructive emotions. However, Stoicism does not seek to suppress emotions or to eliminate them, only to transform them into actions for the greater good.

Action is another principle of Stoicism. Unlike other

philosophical schools, stoicism does not seek to debate about the world around us. This philosophy wants us to take action, take matters into our own hands, and make changes to become stronger and in control of the controllable things.

Stoicism seeks to teach us that the world we are living in is unpredictable, that we have only but a moment given to us to spend on this planet. It also teaches us that it is the logic that will satisfy us and that the cause of dissatisfaction lies in our desire to please our senses. Stoicism is not an intellectual philosophy but a way of life in which we practice logic. It demands training to better ourselves, develop clear judgment, and achieve inner calm.

Like any other philosophy, Stoicism agrees that there is a higher goal in life, known by the Greek term *Eudaimonia*. This term translates as happiness or welfare, but recently, "flourishing," and "prospering" are being proposed as more accurate terms. In various philosophies, personal prospering is the path to happiness. Stoicism is no different. Where it separates from other philosophies is in how to achieve this happiness. Also, while other philosophies often digress from the topic of *Eudaimonia*, Stoicism concentrates almost exclusively on it.

I. WHAT THE HECK IS STOICISM? | 3

To achieve *Eudaimonia*, stoics believe that personal virtue is necessary and the only important thing. *Eudaimonia* is only accessible if you are in perfect balance with your inner "*daimon*". *Daimon* is the Greek word for inner spirit or a divine spark that we all carry in ourselves. (Do not confuse the term "*daimon*" with demon). This balance is only possible if you are the best version of yourself. If you are a person that likes to improve and build yourself consistently, you are aware that what you are striving for is this image of your perfect self. In short, the main principle of Stoicism is the achievement of happiness through the balance between your ideal self and your inner spirit. Ancient Stoics believed that it is in human nature to strive for perfection, and that is why the *daimon*, the divine spark, was planted in us. Like a seed, the *daimon* grows into a human, and it is only natural to grow into the best version of yourself.

But there is always a gap between "what we are" and "what we could be." We strive to close this gap, and we can only do it by *arete*, a Greek term for virtue, which can also be translated as "excellence of character". However, *arete* has a broader meaning as it represents the notion of fulfilling one's purpose and the act of living up to one's potential. Ancient Stoics believed that through *arete*, we would be able to achieve a state of balance with our *daimon*, which will lead to *Eudaimonia*. Through virtue, we will be able to become the best version of ourselves and achieve complete happiness.

In Stoicism, happiness is not just a transitory mood, as many people see it today. *Eudaimonia* is a term that describes happiness as the quality of someone's personal life. It's a condition where a person lives continuously happy, through constant work to better himself. A Stoic's actions are always reflecting his virtue and his best image of his persona. No matter what are the surrounding events that will influence our lives, we must always act with virtue, as that image of the best version of ourselves would do. But how is this possible when life gets tough?

Life is not a smooth ride, and anyone with some experience under their belt will acknowledge how many punches and kicks they've received from life itself. Unexpected things can happen, and they can have a very negative impact on our lives. All our dreams can be shattered in an instant. It is on us alone to not allow any situation to disturb our general happiness, our quality of life, our *Eudaimonia*. Stoics deal with the ways of achieving this happiness. Still, they are not blind to the unexpected things that can happen and ruin our *Eudaimonia*. Stoicism teaches us how to deal with whatever life throws at us. No matter what happens in our life, we must be ready to face it, and we must be prepared not to allow it to extinguish the flame of our *daimon*. But these defense skills must be learned.

If something negative happens to you right at this moment, chances are you'll react very emotionally. You will either panic, be angry or sad. Through practice, you will be able to recognize the emotion but not allow it to disturb your perfect flow of life. Strong emotions are often regarded as weaknesses in Stoicism because they will pollute our happiness if we let them. Emotions are never to dictate our behavior. We must always act in virtue, looking up to that image of the best possible versions of ourselves. Negative emotions are the root of all human suffering as they lead us to irrational behavior and block our *Eudaimonia*.

People are miserable because they are slaves to their emotions. They are unable to control themselves in certain situations, and they give in to weakness too easily. This weakness will make us behave on levels that are very much beneath what we are capable of, and the perfection we should strive for. Stoics then state that if we want to continue enjoying *Eudaimonia*, we need to keep our emotions in check. We need to tame our passions, learn how to control them, and they will have no influence on our life. When we are emotionally resilient, there is nothing that life can throw at us that will disturb our happiness.

Imagine yourself as a warrior; you won't flee the battlefield just because the opponent is fighting back. No, you will give your best to overpower your opponent and win the battle. It is the same with Stoicism; it will provide us with the weapons we need to fight the negative things in our life. We will not flee from what life throws at us, but we'll be well-prepared to fight back and not allow it to destroy us.

Now let's look into another Greek word, which you might be more familiar with. *Apatheia*, a word from which the English word "apathy" comes from. However, the meaning of the Greek term is not equal to its modern derivative. While apathy has a negative connotation as it is a state of indifference, *apatheia* is a state of mind in which passions or strong emotions, cannot disturb us. The best translation for *apatheia* would be equanimity, psychological stability in which we remain undisturbed by emotions, pain, or anything else that can throw our minds out of balance.

When we look at the term *apatheia* knowing its true meaning, we can only observe it as a virtue, a tool for achieving a happy life. For Stoics, it is irrational to react emotionally to external events as we cannot influence those events. What we can do is control ourselves, our minds. Everything external comes from other people's will or nature, and this is something we do not control. To continue being happy, we must control ourselves and respond to the external events in the most virtuous way we are capable of.

Apatheia is in some way similar to Nirvana from Hinduism, as it represents total control of the emotions which will not be allowed to dictate our behavior. However, this does not mean Stoics are suppressing their feelings or trying to get rid of them. Stoics are very capable of feeling, but they can react through logic rather than through emotion. Feelings are ok as long as you do not give in to your passions and let them control your behavior, which will always be irrational.

It is critical to realize that Stoicism does not advise hiding your emotions or trying not to feel. Many people are against Stoicism because they think it's about suppressing one's emotions. They are wrong; Stoics are aware that it is impossible not to feel anything if you are a healthy human being. Stoicism is more about acknowledging your emotions, being aware of how they make you feel, reflecting on their source, on what causes them. Then, learning how to respond to the given situation in a way that will not disturb our lives. It is not about getting rid of emotions, as it is about learning how to control them, and how to tame them.

When we become emotional and let our passion cloud our judgment, it is as if we put a wild beast in control of us. If angry, the wild beast will pull us into unwanted behavioral patterns where we will kick, scream, and destroy anything around us. The wild beast will take control over us and draw us into a cycle of destruction while we blindly follow. Stoics conclude that we are capable of fighting back, of pulling in the other direction than the wild beast chose for us.

With training and practice, Stoicism will allow us to remain calm when we feel angry, to be brave when we are afraid, and to keep going when we are in pain. Being a Stoic is not the same as dismissing emotion; we do not pretend that feelings don't exist. We are capable of taming the wild beast, so the next time it is confronted with strong emotions, it can only snarl and howl, but it won't be able to act. We will be the ones in control, and the beast will have to follow us blindly. Even though it might show the tendency to act up again as an animalistic response to emotion, we do not have to give in; we are in control.

You might ask yourself, what about love? Isn't love a positive emotion, and do Stoics act with love at all? You must understand that it is because Stoics do love that they are bettering themselves. Stoics love their partners, friends, and family members. For the good of the relationship between them, they cannot act passionately but, instead, enjoy love with a calm and rational approach. Stoics don't have a heart of stone; they are capable of feeling all ranges of emotions. They simply don't allow emotions to overwhelm them and destroy their happiness. Stoics often say how they love all humanity, and it is their goal to be useful to all humans, to help others, and to take care of their loved ones. They can achieve all these things only if they are in control of their emotions and if their behavior is that of virtue. Just as you cannot call someone brave if he or she didn't face the peril, you wouldn't call someone Stoic if he or she didn't face his or her emotions. Stoicism is not about eliminating passions or emotions; it's about facing them and learning to control them.

Stoics are sometimes incorrectly seen as too serious, even grim people. But Stoicism is actually quite a joyful philosophy. By acting with virtue and excellence of character, the result is *Eudaimonia*. In *Eudaimonia*, we find fulfillment, living a life undisturbed by the events we cannot control. In *Eudaimonia*, we leave no room for panic, fear, insecurity, or any kind of irrational behavior. What remains in us is pure tranquility. One could say that tranquility is a by-product of Stoicism, as it is not the initial goal. Still, it comes naturally once we consistently act with virtue.

Tranquility is very much appreciated in today's hectic world. It would be amazing to feel strong and confident in all aspects of our lives, and this is what tranquility will allow. But what is tranquility exactly? The old Greek philosophers used to refer to it as *euthymia*, or knowing your path. *Euthymia* is a feeling that overcomes us when we fully trust ourselves. When your actions reflect your values, you will be truly convinced you are doing the right thing. You will be confident and brave, and no one will be able to persuade you otherwise.

Tranquility is the peace of mind that comes with the confidence we have in ourselves. It will come to us only if we are living our lives following the image of the best version of ourselves. People who give in to their passions, who are ruled by their emotions, cannot achieve tranquility. Because they feel insecure, they cannot make logical, rational decisions and are torn between their desires and things they despise. Stoicism will bring you calmness, which will furthermore help you live up to your potential. No matter what life throws at you, you will remain calm and confident. You will know you are taking the best possible action to continue living in *Eudaimonia*, in happiness.

The History of Stoicism

With interest in Stoicism, there comes the interest in its history as well - at least for me. It is only natural to wonder where it all began, and how did philosophers come up with all of this? Who was the first that started it all? To answer these questions, we will dive into a short history of Stoicism.

The father of Stoicism is considered to be Zeno of Citium (334bc-262bc), a merchant from Cyprus who, at the age of 42, found himself in Athens where he met the famous Cynic philosopher Crates of Thebes. Immediately Zeno became his student. There is even a legend that tells the story of how Zeno got interested in philosophy. While on his merchant route, Zeno suffered a shipwreck somewhere between Greece and Cyprus, in the Mediterranean Sea. He found his way to Athens, where he often visited book stores. He was attracted to the work of Socrates, and on one occasion, he asked the owner of the shop where he could find such a person. The bookstore owner pointed at Crates the Cynic, who just happened to pass by the store. Zeno was attracted to the teachings of the Cynics, which helped him realize that philosophy was his true calling.

Indeed, Zeno, the founder of Stoicism, began as a Cynic; however, he extended the teachings, softening its harsh principles and making it more useful and practical. After Crates, Zeno tried being a student of some other philosophers before deciding to open his school. He was known as an ascetic (abstinent). He could not afford the schoolroom, so he began teaching at *Stoa Poikile*, the famous colonnade located in the Athens city center.

At first, his students were known as Zenonians, but to avoid creating the cult of the person, Zeno forbade it. Instead, they started calling themselves Stoics by the *Stoa Poikile*, where Zeno held his classes. Gradually, Stoics abandoned the asceticism that Cynics preached and started enjoying simple comforts in order to live happy lives. Stoics believed their philosophy was to be practiced in day to day life. It would help them conquer life's challenges and make them better humans who would continue caring about other people and nature. And even though they allowed themselves simple pleasures, they claimed they did not cling to them, and would be happy without them too. However, if they were already born in the palace, why not make the best of it? This attitude made Stoicism popular at the time. It brought the teaching to the courts and the higher class of society.

Even after the death of Zeno, Stoicism continued to be the leading philosophy branch in Athens. In 155, Diogenes of Babylon was among the representatives of Athens for the political negotiations with conservative Rome. This way, Stoicism spread from Greece to Rome, where it continued to thrive under the influence of great Stoics such as Cato, Seneca, Epictetus, and Marcus Aurelius.

Stoicism was considered somewhat like a "street philosophy" contrary to the cold, official, academic philosophies. The people readily embraced it. It was available to everyone as anyone could attend the classes. Ultimately, becoming famous among both rich and poor, the powerful and those who suffered, as they all shared a common goal - a good, happy life.

For over five centuries, Stoicism ruled the philosophy scene, and it even influenced early Christianity. However, after the death of its Roman teachers, it started its decline. Stoicism was never forgotten, however, as its ideas continued to live by infiltrating other schools of philosophy. It was resurrected in its full glory in the 20th century when psychiatry gained popularity. It shares so many ideas and exercises with various schools of psychiatry, that it was only natural humans would once more show the interest in this ancient discipline.

. . .

The Stoic Philosophers

To know the history of Stoicism, to fully understand it, it is of great help to learn who the ancient Stoic teachers were, what kind of people they were, and what moved them to become Stoics. It is through their writings and teachings that Stoicism survived through the centuries. These figures are not just of great interest to modern philosophers, but also historians, anthropologists, politicians, artists, and ordinary people who want to better themselves. It would take an entirely separate book to write about all the famous Stoics. Still, by exploring a select few, we can gain a pretty clear picture of how these people used to live, and how they developed Stoicism.

Cleanthes of Assos (330 - 232 BC)

We have already discussed the father of Stoicism, Zeno. Therefore we will skip his story as it is already familiar, but focus on one of his disciples instead.

Cleanthes was not just one of Zeno's students, but also his heir. He became head (scholarch) of the Stoic school after Zeno's death. However, before he showed any interest in philosophy, Cleanthes was a boxer, a profession that led him to Athens, where he heard Zeno speaking for the first time. After taking the role of the school head, Cleanthes was successful in preserving and further developing Zeno's teachings.

Cleanthes was an innovative philosopher when it came to Stoic physics, the principals of materialism, and pantheism. His works are preserved mostly in fragments, the largest one being his "Hymn to Zeus." He developed the theory of tension in Stoic physics, distinguishing materialism from all other concepts of matter, which regarded it as dead and inert. He continued developing his materialism theories by applying them to Stoic logic and ethics.

He thought that the soul was of a material substance. To prove it, he argued that it is visible in genetics where parents not only transfer their physical characteristics but those of the mind as well. He also tried to prove the unity of body and soul by acknowledging that when the body is in pain, so is the soul. When the soul is suffering anxiety, our bodies suffer too. In Stoic physics, fire is regarded as a divine thing that animates all living beings. Because the sun is an entity that sustains all life on earth, Cleanthes regarded it as a divinity too. As a part of the divine fire that we all carry inside and enables us to live.

When it comes to ethics, Cleanthes followed the usual Stoic premise that passions such as love, grief, and pain are weaknesses. He also emphasized that the worldly pleasures were not merely bad but, in fact, contrary to nature and, therefore, completely worthless.

Chrysippus of Soli (280 - 204 BC)

One of Cleanthes' students, and the third head of the school, Chrysippus, extensively expanded the philosophy's doctrines and principles. His best work was in the areas of logic, the theory of knowledge, ethics, and physics. Chrysippus moved to Athens when his estates were confiscated for the king's treasury. Among his contemporaries, he was well known for his intellect and ability to learn as well as his self-confidence. He was a fruitful writer, writing over 700 works. However, he was often accused of filling his books with the quotes of other philosophers.

Chrysippus was the Stoic who created propositional logic, in which we deal with propositions that may be false or true. We use logical connectors to come to the conclusions. Propositional logic will become a foundation for other branches of logic (first-order logic and higher-order logic).

In epistemology, Chrysippus was relying on empiricism. Like other Stoics, he thought that knowledge is always based on experience which we are getting from our senses. He explained that the senses are carrying messages from the external world to us, which will then make an impression on our soul. For Zeno, this impression was similar to the impression a seal would leave on a wax. For Chrysippus, it was different. He thought that impressions are changing our soul, modifying it based on what external object is acting upon us. Only with this change will come the understanding. He also believed that only if we understand the object that is leaving the impression on our soul, we will be able to name it. Until then, we remain ignorant. People use memory, classification, and comparison to distinguish true from false presentations.

Chrysippus also introduced the concept of Fate in Stoicism. He believed that all things happen because they were destined to. Even if something seems to be an accident, there is a hidden cause behind it that is not revealed to us. The world is united by a chain in which the links are made from a cause upon a cause. This fate belief system was based on the Divine, according to Chrysippus. He proved it by saying that if the Divine does not predetermine the future, then the diviners wouldn't be able to predict it. For him, various omens and portents were natural occurrences that followed certain predetermined events.

Seneca the Younger (4 BC - 65 AD)

Lucius Annaeus Seneca often called the Younger to differ from his father, who was a rhetoric Seneca the Older. Seneca was not just a Stoic philosopher but also a statesman, dramatist, and a teacher to young Nero. When Nero became emperor, Seneca became one of his most trusted advisors. It is believed that because of his influence, the government of the first five years of Nero's reign was competent. However, Seneca lost his influence over Nero. When he was 65 years old, Nero ordered him to take his own life because he was suspected of being part of a conspiracy to assassinate the Emperor.

His calmness and serenity in this situation became a legend. The scene where he commits suicide has been depicted by various artists and entered many books, historical or fictional. As a writer, Seneca is known for his philosophical work as well as for his tragedies.

He also wrote 124 letters that dealt with various moral issues. They are known as the *Epistulae Morales ad Lucilium* as they were addressed to Lucilius, a dear friend of his, who was a procurator of Sicily. This persona is known to history only through Seneca's letters, which were written with a broader audience in mind. When read as a collection, the letters form something closer to a diary that deals with themes such as the contempt towards death, the virtue of supreme good or nobility of the wise sage.

Seneca concentrated his Stoic work on ethics, but he also provided one book that deals with the Stoic physics (*Naturales Quaestiones*). He built his philosophical work on the teachings of others, mostly Greek Stoics, and he often quoted Zeno, Cleanthes, and Chrysippus. Seneca is widely known and is commonly referred to as the world's most interesting Stoic because he focused his philosophy on practical things. He often wrote of everyday troubles and how to use stoic wisdom to deal with them. These topics include things such as: friendship, traveling, wealth, poverty, extravagance, illness, anger, grief, death, and more. He even wrote about how to handle yourself while taking your own life.

Seneca was one of the wealthiest people in Rome. Because he dared to speak about happiness in poverty, he was often considered to be a hypocrite. He claimed that external possessions did not matter, and people should not have any interest in them. However, he enjoyed all the riches and vast amounts of wealth he had. Hypocrite or not, Seneca lived a very productive life. His letters are still quoted, millennia after his death, and through them, he still influences Stoicism and the world today.

Epictetus (55 AD - 135 AD)

A person who rose from a slave to a renowned teacher of Stoicism, Epictetus, was born in Phrygia (today's Turkey). His contemporaries mentioned that he was physically lame. Still, it is unknown if it was a birth defect or an injury that caused his lameness. His real name is unknown as he took the name Epictetus, which in Latin means "gained" or "property." He grew up as a slave in Rome, where he was eventually bought by a wealthy freedman (former slave) who worked as a secretary to Emperor Nero. Seeing the bright mind of Epictetus, his owner allowed him to study philosophy, and he chose Stoicism under the tutorship of the famous Roman teacher Musonius Rufus.

After the death of Nero, Epictetus gained his freedom and started his stoic school. However, Emperor Domitian banned philosophy in Rome and banished all the philosophers residing in the city. Epictetus was forced to leave his city and start a school in Nicopolis, Greece. After the death of Domitian, he was invited back to Rome, but he declined, preferring to stay in Nicopolis. Because he was so well known for his talent for rhetoric, students didn't mind traveling to him from all over the Roman Empire to attend his classes. It is said that even Emperor Hadrian went on occasion to listen to Epictetus' classes at his school.

Epictetus didn't write any of his thoughts down. However, he had an eager student, Arrian, who took notes of his classes and published them under the title "Discourses." This is how we have Epictetus' lectures preserved. From these notes, we can see that the favorite teachings of Epictetus were those on how to deal with hardship in life.

Epictetus lived with only a few possessions, and this fact reflected in his teachings. He claimed that we could not possess anything over which we do not have direct control. If something is stolen from us, it is because we did not possess it in the first place. If we had possessed it, it could not have been stolen. The only thing we possess by Epictetus is an opinion or thought. It is the only thing over which we have full control. He further stated that emotional reactions are opinions, such as crying or laughing. Misfortune, argument, and complaints are also opinions over which we can take control. Epictetus teaches that good and evil are in the control of the choice; therefore, it is under our power to be good or evil. Because we are in control, we can achieve total peace of mind no matter what condition of life we are experiencing at the moment.

Marcus Aurelius (121 AD - 180 AD)

Probably the most famous and well-known Stoic was Emperor Marcus Aurelius, who ruled over the Roman Empire. He is known as the last of the "Five Good Emperors." That is, Roman emperors who deserve respect because of their excellent governing. Marcus Aurelius wasn't born as an heir to the previous emperor. He was adopted by Antoninus Pius, who, in turn, was adopted by emperor Hadrian when he lost his nephew and heir. Marcus Aurelius started learning philosophy under various Greek and Roman teachers once he entered the palace life as an heir. However, it was the "Discourses" written by Epictetus that made an impression on young Marcus, and he continued his studies in Stoicism.

The only work of Marcus Aurelius on Stoicism is his book "Meditations." However, he never intended to publish this book; it was more of a personal diary written for no one but himself. Even the title "Meditations" is not his. The book never had a title to begin with. It was later when being published that the book was assigned this title. Yet this book is still considered one of the most influential works on Stoicism. Many international leaders mention it as their favorite book, among them, being Bill Clinton.

The main thoughts exercised in the book are how important it is to analyze the judgment of self and others, and how to develop a cosmic perspective. Stoic ideas Marcus Aurelius shared in his "Meditations" are about avoiding sensory pleasures. He saw them as obstacles that needed to be overcome to be free from the pains and pleasures of the material. He also claimed that a person could only be harmed if they allow their reaction to gain control over their reason. Only through rationality can someone live in total harmony with *logos*, or the notion of reason that pervades the universe. This will allow humankind to rise above the perceptions of good or evil, which is out of our control. Marcus Aurelius also claimed that people have no control over things such as fame or health. Therefore, they are irrelevant, and they are neither good nor bad.

Modern Stoicism

The practice of Stoicism began its revival at the end of the twentieth century, under the name "Modern Stoicism." This term is used for the adjustments made to the ancient philosophy to fit the modern age. Stoicism was revived due to the inspiration modern cognitive psychotherapy drew from the philosophy. It particularly influenced cognitive behavioral therapy where the quote from Epictetus' "Discourses" is still in use: "It's not the events that upset us, but our judgments about the events."

The Swiss "rational persuasion" school of psychotherapy was heavily influenced by Stoicism.

Its founder, neurologist Paul DuBois, often advised his patients to read passages from the writings of Seneca.

From the area of psychotherapy, Stoicism found its way into the broad population where it was received with great respect. Today the philosophy has caught the eye of many world leaders, politicians, artists, and entrepreneurs.

Modern scientific achievements have shifted our view on nature. Because of it, the Stoics views are somewhat hard to uphold in the present times. The Stoics of ancient Greek and Rome believed that you need to live in consistency with nature to have a good life. According to them, nature is by default good; therefore, everything which was in its consistency was also good. Also, Stoics believed that everything in the universe was organized in a rational way to fulfill the ultimate purpose. It was a theological view of the universe that modern-day society doesn't have anymore.

Today, we are aware that the universe is indifferent towards us, and we are very much unimportant to it. It doesn't have a secret plan for our lives and no aim for us to go for. Because the universe is nature according to the old Stoic teachings, we cannot apply them fully today. Some modern philosophers agree that Stoicism today should discard its ties to "nature," however, the philosophy is traditionally tied too much to the term. What we should do today is redefine the term "nature" and interpret it with modern views.

Instead, in modern Stoicism, nature means fact, or better yet fact about the physical world that surrounds us. To follow nature to live happy lives, we need to acquire facts about the world, society, and the situations we are experiencing. Then we need to face those facts and accept them for what they are. We are not to seek higher meaning and ask the questions of why something is happening. The truth is that it is happening, and that is the knowledge we need to draw normative conclusions. However, not all modern Stoics see nature as facts, simply because, in today's world, science is progressing quickly, and everything is subject to change. Therefore, Nature for them is rational, and if we live our lives in accordance with reason, then we will be truly happy. We will develop the Stoic principle of nature even more in the next chapter.

"What then is that which is able to conduct a man? One thing and only one, philosophy. But this consists in keeping the daemon within a man free from violence and unharmed, superior to pains and pleasures, doing nothing without purpose, nor yet falsely and with hypocrisy, not feeling the need of another man's doing or not doing anything; and besides, accepting all that happens, and all that is allotted, as coming from thence, wherever it is, from whence he himself came."

— MARCUS AURELIUS,
MEDITATIONS

II. STOICISM KEY PRINCIPLES

As its building blocks, the principles of Stoicism are what the philosophy is made out of. To see the larger picture of Stoicism is essential to understand what its main principles are and how we define them. We already mentioned them in the first chapter while explaining what Stoicism is. Now it is time to go deeper and explain each of the principles in detail and to explain their use in today's world. However, all building blocks need pillars to support the structure, and it is the same with this particular philosophy. The so-called pillars of Stoicism lie in the understanding of what logic, physics, and ethics are, and how this particular philosophy explains them.

. . .

Logic

While explaining the primary goal of Stoicism and how to achieve it, we often say that Stoics act in a rational, logical way rather than through their emotions. But what is logic to Stoics? How did they perceive it and explain it? But, let's first see what the word logic actually means. Keep in mind that Stoics were not the ones who came up with the term, nor were they the only branch of philosophy who used it.

Logic comes from Greek word *Logos*, which is often translated as "reason." Still, it can also carry the meaning: word, plea, speech, discourse, account, etc. Each branch of ancient Greek philosophy interpreted the word in a way it would suit their teachings. It is believed that the term was first used in Western philosophy to explain the principle of order and knowledge. However, in the end, it all comes down to logic being a study of the reason, and this study is trying to explain what is good reasoning and what is bad reasoning.

Stoics used the term Logic to refer not only to reason but to rhetoric, grammar, propositions, perception, and concepts. However, let's concentrate on reason for a while as this is the area modern

Stoicism follows the old Greek forefathers of philosophy. For Stoics, logic claims the certainty of knowledge. And this certainty can only be achieved if the conviction is verified by peers and by the collective judgment of others. Stoics believe that humans are bombarded by sensations all the time, and these sensations leave various impressions on us. Our minds are capable of approving or rejecting the impression, and by doing so, the mind is capable of distinguishing true or false representations of reality. However, once we are aware, which representation of reality is true, that does not immediately mean we know of it. The only thing we are left with is an impression.

Knowledge is more complex for Stoics. It is a system of approved impressions which will become unshakable and secure from other opinions and other reasoning. This sense of knowledge is available only to the very few who manage to live their lives in complete accordance with their *Eudaimonia*. Stoics set the bar for knowledge very high, and they are willing to accept that knowledge is not the rule, but more of an exception. It was perfectly fine to admit they did not have it.

A person who possesses knowledge was called a

Stoic Sage. Everyone else was ignorant. Stoicism leaves no room for the people who would be part of the third category, which would take place in between wise and ignorant. They dealt with the extremes only. If you did not achieve *Eudaimonia*, you are still ignorant, and you have to continue working on bettering yourself.

Physics

The word physics might sound a bit intimidating to some people. The first thing that comes to mind when we hear it is equations, string theory, gravity, atoms, space travel, time travel, and so on. However, in philosophy, physics is not about the observable laws of nature that can be demonstrated and proven. We are too used to thinking in a materialistic way. We see our world as a solid matter that can be touched or felt.

Stoics were not materialists but were often called physicalists. For example, the concept of the body is completely different now than what it used to be for Stoics. While we see the body as something that occupies a three-dimensional space that affects and can be affected by other entities, a Stoic body is more than that. They saw thoughts, emotions, and the soul as physical parts of the body. For the ancient Stoics, the body wasn't just that, a material object. It also embodied the principles of all that is Active and Passive, the Universe itself, and reason. All these intangible things are physical to Stoics, and they tried to explain them through what is known as Stoic physics.

Stoics pursued physics in order to understand the world as a coherent entity. Because of this, their physics can be described as monism (they believed the universe is the one almighty God). Materialism (they believed that abstract qualities like wisdom, soul, or emotions were corporeal). And dynamism (everything that exists is active and passive, it can act and be acted upon).

Ethics

Stoicism is based on Cynicism from which it borrowed a premise that good lies in the state of the soul, in wisdom and self-control. However, they expanded their philosophy and started teaching that freedom from passion and freedom from weaknesses is achieved by following reason.

For the ancient world, the word passion didn't have the same meaning it has today. Passions were strong emotions with a negative connotation like anger, anguish, or pain. This is why passions were seen as weaknesses and why one must get rid of them. However, getting rid of the passions didn't mean extinguishing all emotions. Stoics sought to transform them through *askesis*, which would clear their judgment. However, Stoics do not refer to the modern concept of asceticism in which people deprive themselves of all pleasure. For Stoics, it was more about moral asceticism, only doing what is morally right. Asceticism today is abstinence from all worldly pleasures. In contrast, for Stoics, those pleasures are indifferent, and they are not to be pursued as something purely good.

Because they are indifferent, pleasures are neither good nor bad. As a Stoic, you are allowed to enjoy whatever pleasures you may see fit as long as you are ready to make a morally good decision at any given time. This type of ascesis where the pleasures are of no importance will bring you clear judgment and inner calm.

Unhappiness and evil are the results of our ignorance towards nature; it is the lack of reason itself. If your behavior is unkind, it is because you are ignorant of your universal reasoning. This ignorance would lead you to the conclusion that being cruel is your necessary response to a particular circumstance. Remember that we cannot affect anything that comes from the outside, we can only control ourselves; therefore, to control our behavior. To succeed in this, one must examine his own judgment and determine what the cause of his behavior is. Once found, the cause can be overcome, and the person will be in perfect balance with nature, which will allow him to correct his or her behavior.

Nature

Nature plays a significant role in Stoicism. It is the first building block of the philosophy as its founders taught that living in accordance with nature is the only way of living a happy life. However, this ancient Stoic ideal is somewhat confusing to modern Stoics. We already explained that the old definition of Nature does not apply to the present time, but we cannot discard this traditional ideal of Stoicism. We need to come to new conclusions of what nature is today, and how we can live in accordance with it.

There is a trap in this ancient Stoic saying, "live in accordance with nature." It appeals to us as humans, and we might think it's so simple, yet wise. It is because simple quotes that generalize things are appealing to our emotions, and this is what we should avoid. We need to ask ourselves what nature is in this case, and through its meaning, we will achieve understanding. However, there is no simple and straightforward answer to the question of what nature is for the Stoics today. Many have tried to give their own solutions, but not all will agree with them simply because this is a complicated question, and there are no correct simple answers to it.

For the ancient Greek and Roman Stoics, nature was seen through theology. Nature was the universe, or cosmos, if you prefer, and it was divine. We already discussed why this classic concept of nature does not apply to us living in the present time. We, as humans, living in the modern world, tend to seek answers closer to ourselves. This is why modern Stoics narrowed the question of nature to what it means to live in accordance with HUMAN nature. Now it looks like the answer to the problem might be more straightforward. However, what exactly is human nature? Let's see how classical Stoics explain this term, to begin with.

Classical Stoics tried to give an answer to human nature by comparing it with animal nature. The first impulse of an animal, for example, is self-preservation. The early Stoics broadened the concept of self-preservation to all living things, even plants. The ancient Stoics thought that it is nature that drove all living things, and it did not make any difference between plants, animals, and humans. This is why we all have that vegetative part of us, the part without impulses and sensations. However, by nature, plants are unable to move; therefore, they cannot act in accordance with nature. Animals and humans, however, can and do. For both animals and humans, it is in their nature to follow this impulse of self-preservation.

And now we come to the difference between animals and humans. The difference is that by nature, humans are given better leadership that will bring them to self-preservation, and that is their ability to reason. Therefore, reason becomes the natural life. By living with reason, living rationally, we live in accordance with nature.

Humans don't just possess the ability to reason as the sole vehicle that will lead us blindly to self-preservation. We also have the capacity to change or reshape our impulses. We can react to the environment we are living in by acting upon our impulses. But we are also capable of handling the impulses themselves, and most importantly, controlling our actions. It is done by taking an active role in the society we are living in and bettering ourselves through constant improvement, through virtue.

Virtue

What Stoics have in mind when they say that living in accordance with nature is done through virtue, they are talking about a similar concept to the medieval honor code. Stoics never had an honor code by or in itself; however, they did say that living honorably is what living in accordance with nature is all about.

Stoics came to the conclusion that there are four main virtues to live by:

1. Wisdom (*sophia*)
2. Righteousness (*dikaiosune*)
3. Fortitude (*andreia*)
4. Temperance (*sophrosune*)

In modern Stoicism, these terms were translated as: wisdom, justice, courage, and self-discipline. Stoics did not randomly choose the virtues they thought simply sounded the best, or are easiest to follow. In fact, when looked at the wider picture, these virtues are appreciated by the majority of cultures and religions across the whole world. Because of this, they are considered universal virtues, natural to humans.

One person can be better at some virtues than others. You might be good at self-discipline, but you wouldn't say you are very courageous. However, for Stoics, it is not enough to be amazing at only one or two virtues. They are a package and come as a whole, and you must practice living within all of them. This is why we cannot call a courageous thief a man of virtue just because he has courage. He obviously lacks wisdom, justice, and self-discipline to some extent; therefore, he is not a virtuous person, and he cannot be a Stoic.

Ancient Stoics were aware that it would take a long time to practice all the virtues to perfection, and this is something that is achievable only by the Sages. However, living the life of constant practice is already good enough, as overcoming your emotions and living to the best extent of your persona is what makes you a Stoic or a virtuous person. Trying to be the best version of yourself, and making progress day by day is what counts. It is the effort, not the goal that is important for the Stoic. Imperfections are natural for Stoics; however, that doesn't mean we should ignore them. We should continuously observe them, analyze them, see where they are coming from, and then make rational decisions on how to improve them.

In summary, then, here are the four virtues and how we can balance their practice in our lives. This is how we become a Stoic; by being aware of these universal virtues, and constantly working to improve ourselves within their framework:

1. Wisdom is all about understanding which actions are appropriate for a given situation. It includes debate, sound judgment, a clear perspective, and good sense. Only when you can come up to a rational conclusion, using the tools of wisdom, you can be virtuous.
2. Justice is knowledge of how to act in relationships with others. Justice is fairness, having integrity, and doing a service to the public. It is about the ability to perceive

others and their actions with a clear mind, without prejudice and with sympathy.

3. Courage is acting correctly in situations that generally cause fear. It is not about not feeling fear, but knowing how to respond to it. It is about being persistent no matter what the difficulties are. It is about having confidence that will allow you to face your fears without difficulties.
4. Self-discipline is acting correctly despite the emotions you are experiencing. It is conquering and taking control of emotions such as desire, lust, anger, desperation, and anything else that brings nothing but negativity. Self-discipline is about having order, taking control, forgiving, and being humble.

Now that you understand the main principles of Stoicism let's discuss how they relate to the Stoic's way of life.

Attention

What we today consider mindfulness, the Stoics of classical times called *prosoche*, which translates to attention. Attention will help us be aware of all our stages in life in which we are the best versions of ourselves. The goal is to perform a given task in the best possible way we can. In order to do so, we must be aware of all the aspects of the task at hand and give them all equal, vigorous attention. It is just like solving a puzzle; you have to give each piece of the puzzle the same attention in order to make a decision where to place them in order to solve the puzzle. This is exactly the attention Stoicism demands for whatever action we are pursuing.

To actively align our actions with virtue, we have to focus our attention and learn how to use self-observation. How else would we possibly act with virtue if we are not even aware of what we are doing? If our minds keep wandering, we are far away from being the best version of ourselves. We are far from achieving *Eudaimonia*, and we keep drifting away from it the more we allow distractions to overcome us. It is precisely here that mindfulness comes to help. Being aware that we are not paying attention is the first step in bettering our actions. Catch yourself when your mind is wandering, and you will be able to correct it. Without attention, our actions will become impulsive, automatic, random, and not in accordance with nature.

This is exactly the opposite of what Stoicism teaches us.

Epictetus warned his students that losing attention today will affect their lives tomorrow. He continued explaining that it is not so simple to regain attention once lost. In fact, losing attention leads to the creation of a bad habit of not paying attention further in life. This is how we fall into an endless cycle of postponing and procrastinating. Being distracted is living on the opposite side of nature because we will not be able to recall the attention to reason. By losing attention, we are allowing our instincts to take over our control and lead us away from the happy life. Epictetus also mentions how just as we are paying attention to avoid stepping on a sharp object and hurt ourselves, the Stoic should always be mindful not to harm the ruling faculty of his own mind and relapse into the vice. Losing attention is abandoning the present moment, and that means we'd become mindless.

Character

Epictetus taught his followers that the only way to recognize a true Stoic is by his character. Classical

Stoics thought that looks are indifferent, and it's the character of someone that should represent a person in its best light. No matter what social circle you are coming from, what is your role in the community, how you dress, or how you walk, the only thing that matters is your character. However, is this principle of old still valid in our times when beauty and status are the measure of everything in our modern society? Each hour we are bombarded by commercials, movies, music, and so on, which program us to believe that beauty, money and fame are the end-all-be-all. But is this really true, or does it just appear to be true?

Modern Stoicism still believes that the ultimate goal is excellence of character. Just think of the person you admire the most and ask yourself what do you admire in that person? It can be a relative, parent, friend, lover, or actor; it doesn't matter. You will notice that the things that we admire when it comes to someone are mostly their inner characteristics, not their looks or possessions. You can admire a person because he is a trustworthy friend, honorable in judgment, he is consistent in his actions and honest even when it is inconvenient to him. When you think of a person's inner value, it becomes obvious why Stoics appreciate character over appearances. All the traits you admire in your friend are virtues, and they really are the ultimate good in Stoicism. Virtues will shape you into a good person, and this can bring some extra bonuses like career promotion, the admiration of your peers, the love of your close ones, and so on. These bonuses will fill your life with joy, and you will feel worthy as you are playing your role in society.

Be careful, for these bonuses that come with being virtuous are not the goal. You should act with virtue because that is the right thing to do. The extra benefits will bring you happiness and joy, but these are irrelevant feelings. Of course, Stoicism won't tell you not to allow yourself to experience them. But that to act in a "nice way", thinking of what you might get in return, is not virtuous at all. Virtue in itself is the reward as it is the only right way of living. Think of these bonuses as something that is not under your control. They might come, or they might not. That doesn't mean that your actions are in vain. That one time when you were courageous and stood up to a bully maybe didn't bring you the respect and awe of your peers, but it was still the right thing to do because the bullying stopped and someone else's condition improved.

Marcus Aurelius recognized three types of character which claim to be kind. The first one will ask for a reward or a favor in return once he acts in kindness. The second type will not ask directly for a reward but will think of others as being in their debt. The third type asks for nothing in return when he acts in kindness. His goal is the next kind act he can perform without looking back with expectations. Stoics believe that it is in human nature to do good deeds, and because it is natural, it is reasonable, therefore, the only right way of living.

Social Duty

People often think of Stoics as cold and distant people, but the philosophy of Stoicism couldn't be further from that. In fact, Stoics are paying close attention to nurturing the natural bond humans have with each other. Humans are social beings, and we constantly crave that connection with our peers. Because it is in human nature to be close to other people, it is rational to maintain good relations. This is how Stoics will keep living in accordance with nature. Stoics are filled with kindness; they are gentle people filled with love for humanity. Their goal is to be useful to society or the community they are living in; they love to take care of themselves and the others.

For Stoics, it is only natural to be concerned for other people's well-being, no matter if they are close relatives, strangers, or even rivals. This is because we all share the same world, and we influence each other. How can we be well and live happily if our kin is suffering? Epictetus said that a person could not achieve anything good for himself unless he contributes to a community in some way. It is in human nature to live in a community, and in order for the community to be happy, everyone must take their roles and fulfill their given tasks. Humans are comparable to bees, just like them, we will wither and perish if we are isolated. Another similarity we share with the bees is that they, too, need to work for the hive in order to achieve prosperity. Humans do depend on each other, and Stoicism teaches that the bonds between people are important and need to be nurtured.

Marcus Aurelius explained this love towards others as an action we perform in order to help society. What is good for the community can only bring us benefits as we are part of that same community. We will never be able to express the best version of ourselves unless we do the common good. To be able to reach the very best version of ourselves, we have to work on the well-being of others. Being a social being doesn't mean we need a society just not to feel lonely. The connection between people runs on a much deeper level. We wouldn't survive without each other's help.

Helping others is a virtue, and remember that virtue in itself is a reward. However, there are other aspects to be enjoyed too. If we help others, it is highly possible we will receive help once we need it. This return in favor shouldn't be the goal of our kind actions, but we could enjoy the benefits of it as a secondary result. In this sense, doing good will improve your chances of having a happy life, and there is not a single reason why you shouldn't. It might seem that this could be classified as a selfish reason to do good, and in some way, it is. However, no one will intentionally do good to improve their lives; it is simply another bonus. What matters is that goodness is our nature, and it is rational to do good. Because it is rational, our lives can only be happy, as reason is in perfect accordance with nature.

. . .

The Potential Within Us

As we discussed in the previous sections, it is a natural force that gave us reason, so we can work towards our self-preservation in the best possible way. But nature gave us something else to strive for, and that is the ability to thrive in life. This is why the divine seed, or inner *daimon*, the vision of the best version of ourselves, was planted within us. It is in our natural potential to become the best versions of ourselves. Humans are born with the natural inclination to do good; we all have the natural ability to be virtuous. The seed is within us, and it is now our duty to nurture it and let it reach its highest potential. We were designed, by nature, to live good lives, and it is within our power to make it happen.

Virtue is the perfecting of our nature and living with *arete* (excellence). It is meant to complete our nature. When we are unable to complete our nature and to live by it, we will have unfulfilled lives with a constant feeling that something is missing. That feeling of emptiness is what drives us to better ourselves and to reach our highest potential.

To create a clearer picture, let's look at the following analogy. If you observe a tree, its nature is to grow, and its potential is to give fruits. When in perfect agreement with nature, the tree will fulfill its highest potential. It is the good nature of the tree that will lead it to fulfill its potential of bearing fruits. It is the same with us, in order to reach our highest potential, we must live in agreement with nature, through virtue. Only then will our lives be good enough to allow us to express our highest potential.

There is nothing material that will be required for you to have a good life. No money will buy happiness; you do not need a villa with a pool, or an expensive car. It is the potential within us that is given by nature that drives us forward, and through virtue, we will reach that potential. Everyone can achieve a good life, no matter how they look or how rich or poor they are. The is potential within us all, and we should not look for it in external things.

> "No person has the power to have everything they want, but it is in their power not to want what they don't have, and to cheerfully put to good use what they do have."
>
> — SENECA

III. THE RULER AND THE SUBJECT

For Stoics, reason must be the ruler of emotions, not the other way around. Nonetheless, Stoicism isn't about suppressing your emotions. Stoics have a particular approach to experiencing their emotions; however, they do feel.

Stoics believe that if they live their life well, they will experience joy, peace, and satisfaction. Stoics study and learn what it means to be a human being; therefore, they try to live according to nature and find their place in the world. Indeed, Stoics focus a great deal on matters of the mind; however, that doesn't mean that emotions should be ignored. After all, they are still a significant part of us. Emotions have their own place, even though they aren't the central focus.

Stoics don't allow emotions to become their guides for behavior. Even if you feel negative emotions, you won't act out based on them. If you find yourself yelling in anger at your kids, you should take a step back to realize that your behavior makes no sense. Your anger is never justified, it comes as a result of having a wrong perspective.

Being a Stoic is all about your inner transformation and becoming a better person. Your main goal is to develop yourself into a better human being. For instance, one of your hurdles might be overcoming fear, so you may constantly put yourself in situations that normally cause fear to prevent that emotion from taking you over by surprise. Maybe you also get easily angered by rude people, so you take steps to interact with such people more often to gain control over your anger instead of being overtaken by it. However, being a Stoic isn't only about improving yourself as an individual. A Stoic is also driven to improve his or her surroundings, to somehow improve the human condition itself.

Some people are too driven to better themselves, that they ignore their social duty of improving the lives of others as well. Stoics take their duty seriously, and they take steps to help those who aren't

Stoics to improve themselves as well. For instance, a Stoic might try to teach this path to others so that they can benefit from it. However, this doesn't mean that you should just push your philosophy onto others. You could also help others in fixing some of their daily problems and escape the trouble they find themselves in. Marcus Aurelius is one of the best examples of a Stoic who knew that social duty is a truly important aspect. He sought to bring order and justice to a corrupted society and improve the lives of his fellow Romans.

Two Sides of the Coin

While Stoics don't allow feelings and emotions to cloud their judgment, it doesn't mean that they don't experience them. This philosophy considers three good feelings to be of importance:

1. Joy
2. Wish
3. Caution

They are seen in contrast to the three main passions, which are:

1. Pleasure
2. Lust
3. Fear

Additionally, the feeling of distress is recognized, which doesn't have an opposite. These passions are also referred to as bad feelings in this case.

This might sound strange because who compartmentalizes feelings this way? And by what criteria? Well, to fully understand that we need to penetrate the minds of the ancient Greek Stoics. However, to keep it simple, all of these feelings are categories, and they contain every shade of gray when it comes to human emotion. Envy, sorrow, rage, and everything else you can think of are part of these categories in one way or another.

Stoics know that desiring that which you do not have and can never have, is a waste of time and energy. Lust, sometimes referred to as appetite instead, is considered to be an irrational need to chase that which you don't possess. This is where we can also place greed and define it as an unreasonable hunger for anything material. Enmity is another type of hunger, or appetite, that makes us lust for revenge. All of these emotions sap us of our time, energy, and life force itself because they push us to chase outcomes that won't improve our lives. Happiness cannot be found by running after something that isn't under your control.

Lust tells us that happiness lies in the objects we desire. For the Stoics, the opposite of Lust is Wish. Let's discuss Wish because it may seem like an unusual way of describing a good feeling. Wish is a feeling that, in fact, is quite a different perspective and a change in mentality. Wish, in this case, means that you would like to have something; however, your happiness does not depend on that something. There are many good things to strive for in life. However, finding true happiness in them is not possible. Wish simply offers us the foundation we can use in order to take wise actions.

Fear and Caution work the same way. Fear, the opposite of Caution, can be seen as an irrational anxiety of something you are recognizing as a threat in the near future. This negative feeling blocks our *Eudaimonia*. Caution, however, is all about preparing yourself for the challenges that you will inevitably face because that's life. You must be prepared; however, you still need to understand that peace is not found externally. To blossom in life, we need to hone our awareness to not become anxious about the future, but be prepared.

For the Stoics, seeking Pleasure as an end in itself, is also detrimental to our being and our *Eudaimonia*. Instead of striving for temporary pleasures and instant gratification, we should pursue Joy, which is everlasting.

Mastering Emotion

Have you ever procrastinated? The answer to that is most probably 'yes' because who hasn't, especially in the age of the Internet. Remember a time, maybe recently, when you had to perform an important task, and you really struggled to motivate yourself to complete it. However, no matter what you tried to do, you always ended up switching to YouTube or checking out your Instagram feed. Whenever we have to execute an important task that is really challenging and even stressful, we tend to feel some anxiety and doubt. The reason we end up on YouTube, Netflix, or a social media platform is not because we don't have enough willpower to get the job done. By getting distracted, we are trying to cope with our anxiety and stress. We are trying to hide our negative emotions.

Nobody likes negative emotions. Nobody likes anxiety. The reason for your procrastination isn't the lack of an ability to control your urges. In fact, it's your inability to deal with your negative emotions. This makes look for the nearest escape hatch, and the Internet usually provides it in the form of distracting entertainment that brings you pleasure instead of anxiety.

Emotion regulation is an ability you need to train in order to manage and control your negative emotions. This concept is all about having the ability to handle negative emotions in a healthy, constructive manner. The problem is that we aren't resilient enough to push through the negative experiences, so we seek comfort. If we don't strive to master our emotions, we will dive deeper into a vicious cycle of anxiety, procrastination, depression, and other disorders and addictions.

The Stoics are experts at regulating their emotions and keeping them under control. However, the concept of emotion regulation was perfected only in the 20th century. Before that, the ancient Stoics practiced what is known as reappraisal. This means that you can interpret any kind of event or scenario in such a way that its impact on you will no longer be so negative.

A Stoic who is fully in control of his emotions will be capable of reappraising a situation and eliminate the negative emotions that are associated with it. There comes a time when you have to admit to yourself that you are not in control of any external event and struggling against the tide just prolongs your suffering.

Just think of Seneca. Remember how emperor Nero instructed him to commit suicide because he was suspected of treason by participating in a plot against him? Seneca was a master at controlling his emotions. Once he heard the order from the emperor himself, he knew that he had no other option. His fate was sealed, so he wrote his will, comforted his wife, made peace, and killed himself as ordered.

You might think that he should've fought for every breath, but he had no options. If he hadn't left this world on his own terms, the emperor would've had him killed anyway. This way, fate decided that he needed to die; however, Seneca was still in control of how he was going to die. So, he chose to make peace, finish what he needed to do, and exit the stage courageously.

> "It takes the whole of life to learn how to live, and - what will perhaps make you wonder more - it takes the whole of life to learn how to die."
>
> — SENECA, *ON THE SHORTNESS OF LIFE*

IV. THE STOIC PRACTICES

Stoicism is a practical philosophy, and until now, we learned the theoretical part. In order to properly implement what we learn, we must practice Stoicism. Knowledge itself is not enough, although it is an excellent starting point. Without knowledge, there wouldn't be anything to start practicing. However, implementing Stoicism in the real world is not easy. It is not enough to know its theory and think you are ready to start living a Stoic life tomorrow; it takes time, patience, and practice. In this section of the book, you will learn about the ancient practices of the Stoics and how to incorporate them to your routine.

Philosophy is teaching us how to live a good life. Epictetus compared philosophers to artisans. As a painter uses canvas and paints to make a beautiful piece of art, a philosopher uses his own life as the raw material he will shape into goodness. Observe the events of your life as blank canvases you can use to create a perfect painting. Draw from the experience of the process of painting and learn how to shape your highest potential as a human being. Apply Stoic principles to the real world, put them into real practice, and enjoy the fruits of joy and happiness that will come with the good life you will create for yourself.

A word of advice is needed here. These practices are not to be seen as the infallible way of dealing with specific situations. They are more like guiding lines, and some will work better than others. It is upon you to use your sound judgement in any given scenario and choose the right actions in alignment with your inner voice, your *daimon*. With that approach, you will be able to live a virtuous life and enjoy happiness, independent of the external outcomes of your decisions.

In this chapter, you will learn about preparing practices, the ones you can practice by yourself in the comfort of your home. They will help you understand and master the next set of practices which deal with real problems, specially with other people. Before diving into them, if you learn how to be mindful and don't think of yourself as one of the sages, you will be able to get the most out of the practices.

Acceptance

We already talked about the Stoic view on acceptance and why it is important. Everything external that happens, be it good or bad, is out of your control. Learn to accept it as there is no point in wishing things were different. When we resist reality, we think that life is going against us, and our emotional response would be to fight it. But this is a path to suffering. The reality will be no different, no matter how much we want it to be. There is no other way except acceptance.

Classical Stoics had a saying: "If this is the will of nature, so be it." Stoics of Ancient Greece and Rome believed in fate, in the divine, in a higher force that directs their life. It doesn't matter if you believe in such things, that is entirely up to you. What you must accept is the fact that whatever happens, you have no control over it. The only thing you can control is your actions in response to the external events.

In our day and age, there is a popular prayer that has been widely adopted by Alcoholic Anonymous groups. In its essence, is actually quite Stoic. It's called the "Serenity Prayer", and it goes like this:

God, grant me the Serenity to accept the things I cannot change;

Courage to change the things I can;

and Wisdom to know the difference.

Your acceptance of the external events must not be out of desperation, but natural and willing. Even if people put a label on a situation as bad or evil, the event must be accepted. Only our actions are of importance, and they are the ones we can label as good or bad, evil or righteous. Stoics need to adapt to whatever external events they encounter. Only if we respond with the right actions, nothing will have the power to crush us, to defeat us.

Reality must be accepted, and we should waste no

energy, wondering why the event occurred. Instead, we should focus our energy on where it matters. And as we have said, our power is in virtue by which we can control our actions. You have to accept that you don't get to choose the life you are living, it is given to you, and it is what it is. Yours is to live that life to your highest potential and not resist it. In resistance lies suffering, in acceptance lies prosperity.

Don't confuse the acceptance of external events as passive resignation. Stoics do not resign; they continue working. When we accept reality, we can start improving our condition. We determine with our reason what are the best actions we could take, and we immediately start implementing them.

Here's a popular story, set in a different context and culture, that exemplifies the virtuous Stoic acceptance of an external event. A fireworks manufacturer in China finished his day at the factory and went home to his family to spend the rest of the day with them. Suddenly, there was a loud banging on his door. A neighbor came running, bringing terrible news: His factory was in fire. Because of all the highly flammable materials, firefighters were struggling to extinguish the flames. Instead of giving in to despair, the owner of the factory decided to invite all his neighbors and close friends to watch the show. The place was burning, so all the fireworks were setting off. No one had ever seen such a show in their lives, and they actually enjoyed it. Our factory owner joined his community in enjoying the show his burning factory was producing for them. The next day, with the help of firefighters and neighbors, he started rebuilding his business.

Instead of giving in to despair and suffering, our factory owner did the only thing he could control, and that is to make the best out of such an ugly situation. He did not resign; he started rebuilding his business the very next day. Reality was that his factory was burning, and seeing himself as a victim, or cursing God or fate would be pointless. There was no place in his mind for wishing things were different as it would lead to nothing. There was no room for self-pity. He was aware of where his powers were. In rebuilding!

Foreseeing the Bad

When we act with virtue and according to reason, it is natural to expect good things to happen. However,

IV. THE STOIC PRACTICES | 67

the results that come from our right actions are also out of our control. Our actions must be completed with good intentions, but we have no control over its effects. Many people take precautions to prevent negative outcomes, even Stoics do and that is reasonable. Nevertheless, being aware that things may not go as we planned them, it is also reasonable to prepare for the worst-case scenario. This is where the Stoic exercise of negative visualization comes in handy. It is an imaginative exercise in which you will foresee the negative events. This exercise will prepare you to stay calm no matter how bad the situation is. Staying calm will enable you to act with reason and deal effectively with chaos. Negative visualization is a great exercise to cultivate emotional resilience.

To be calm when facing chaotic situations will help you reflect on it with reason. Reason will allow you to act with virtue, such as courage. You will be able to act in accordance with the best version of yourself. However, to be able to do this, you need to train. By using negative visualization, you will train yourself to be ready to deal with the hard stuff. However, this is not the only benefit you will have from negative visualization. It will allow you to clearly determine your values and to live by your core principles. The exercise itself is quite simple, and you can do it every day.

Before you commit to achieving any particular goal, ask yourself;

1. What could go wrong?
2. What obstacles will I have to overcome?
3. What could be the worst-case scenario?

This is how you will make yourself ready for undesirable outcomes no matter what you are about to do. You can do this exercise from anywhere, sitting at the comfort of your home, being at work, or in school. It is important to practice while things are going well, so you will be prepared when things go downhill. This is how you avoid absolute hell. Prepare for the worst, and if it happens, you will be better equipped to overcome it. Also, you will avoid being shocked and useless when negative events come because you were already expecting them.

You can use this practice not only for life and death scenarios, but for more normal situations as well. Think of going on a date for the first time with a particular woman or man. While you are preparing yourself, think of the obstacles you might encounter.

It could be conversational blocks, or maybe the restaurant will lose your reservation, or you might bump into you ex. There is plenty of stuff that can go wrong on a first date. Visualize them happening and overcoming them. This way, if they do happen in reality, you will be prepared to deal with them in a calm and rational manner that will lead to a better outcome. But to do this exercise, you do not have to wait until your next date. Use your imagination and create such events in your head, just for practice. This way, you make yourself more emotionally resilient in time.

Nonetheless, as with almost everything in life, do not take the negative visualization practice to the extreme and overdo it. Be careful not to allow this form of training to overwhelm you. Set a specific time for it, and then move on to enjoy the rest of your day.

Planning Your Day

Every day, when you wake up, you should take some time to look inside yourself, listen to your inner *daimon*, and plan for the day ahead. This is the Stoic morning practice, which you can easily incorporate to your routine. Stoics often advocate morning planning as the best way to start the day. This practice is as old as the philosophy. Even Epictetus advises his students to do it. The practice is simple, and you can do it while having your morning coffee or tea.

When you wake up and feel comfortable enough, ask yourself: What else can I do to achieve emotional resilience? What else do I need to do to achieve tranquility? Remind yourself that you are a rational being and reflect on the importance of that fact. Do not identify yourself with the corporeal or material things. The point of this exercise is to reflect on the virtues you need to live by, to achieve the tranquility that will help you overcome the obstacles through the day. It will also help if you remind yourself that it is a good thing to be alive. It is a privilege to breathe, think, and love.

Each day is a challenge on its own, and while you are planning for it, do not think only of things to be done, like a checklist. You can also use this morning time to do some negative visualization and prepare your mind for any situation you might encounter. It doesn't matter if you like to plan your day to the smallest detail. What matters is that you train yourself to be aware that your plans are out of your control. Be prepared for unexpected situations that might ruin your plans, and you will have no trouble dealing with the negative change of events if they come.

You can almost be certain someone you will encounter during the day will be a negative or toxic person. The question is, will you be ready for that encounter? Or will you let your emotions take over? If you prepare yourself at the beginning of the day, you will have no problem controlling your emotions and responding rationally to such people. Be aware that people you will meet, no matter how they act, they are your kin, and you should always act with virtue when dealing with them. After all, Stoicism is about love for humanity. If you prepare yourself in the morning, you won't have difficulties showing kindness, empathy, patience, and forgiveness.

It might also find useful to reflect on Seneca's words that nothing is permanent. Not good situations or bad ones. We do not have to fear the negative people or situations as they will leave our lives eventually. On the other hand, we cannot trust the good times as they are not permanent either. All our securities could be destroyed within a minute, our friends might be indisposed, or our loved ones might not give us a helping hand. So, reflect on the passing of everything that now appears so real. In one of the coming exercises, you will learn how the Stoics reflect on the mortality of everything.

Reflecting

In the evening, when the events of the day passed, you should take time to reflect on what's happened. You may want to do it while writing a journal or while meditating. Ask yourself, what did you do during the day? What happened? Was it good or bad? How did you react in a given situation? How can you improve your reaction next time?

You need to reflect on your day each evening to create a habit that will keep you practicing virtue. However, there is a second benefit to repeating the morning and evening practice of planning and reflecting. You will be exercising self-discipline by being consistent with these practices. Reflecting, planning, and self-discipline exercises will give you mental clarity.

Seneca talked about these evening reflecting sessions, as "pleading his case each night at his own court." He remembered his actions and judged them.

This helped him to not repeat his mistakes in the future. By making yourself aware of the mistakes you made during the day, you will realize what needs to change in your behavior. It is like accepting your own advice and moving forward. Don't reflect only on your daily achievements. Pay special attention to the things you failed to do, or you left undone. If it is possible, try to finish or redo those things tomorrow.

By reflecting on the day, you will also gain more control of your negative emotions. Remember, you are a rational being, and don't judge your actions emotionally. Use reason and remember that you did not have control over the external events. If you acted emotionally, take a note of it and change it in the future. There is no reason to be angry if you lashed out in a moment, the moment passed. What you can do is make sure next time a similar situation arises, you will be under control and act reasonably.

This reflection exercise will also contribute to your mindfulness or attention. It is important to make yourself aware of the actions you performed during the day. This way, you will be able to express your highest self whenever possible. If you are not paying attention to your actions, how can you be sure what to improve next time? If you are mindless, you cannot act with virtue, as you don't really know what you are doing. This is the reason why both morning planning and evening reflecting are important to the Stoic routine. They make you aware of who you are and what your actions should be. Only through awareness will you be able to act virtuous and reach the best version of yourself.

Memento Mori

Memento Mori is a Latin proverb which means "remember you will die." It came to a wider use with the rise of Christianity and concepts of heaven and hell. Later, it was used as a symbol in various artistic endeavors. However, Stoics used this proverb since the beginning. It is important to reflect not just of the impermanence of all things, but yourself too. We are all going to perish, and we cannot control it. The only thing that is under our control is the way we chose to live. To make the most out of the time that's been given to us.

Most people fear death; however, for the Stoics, such fear is irrational. Why are we afraid of a perfect constant in our lives as death is? It is all around us, and it is one of the external events we cannot control. Who has not suffered the loss of a friend, family member, or even a pet? People often feel that the death of others is normal. They will grieve over it, as it had to happen one way or another, and people are aware of it. However, when it comes to their own mortality, it is hard to believe that one day they will also seize to exist. It is often so unfathomable that people chose intentionally not to think about it. But not Stoics.

We have to be mindful of our own mortality. Only if we are completely aware of it, we can truly live in accordance with our nature. Living as if it's our last day does not mean we should indulge ourselves in earthly passions and give in to drugs, sexual depravity, extravagance and vice in general. Being aware of your mortality should inspire you to live a quality life — one filled with virtue, love for others, and actions that will reflect the best version of ourselves. To live each day as if it's our last opportunity to act as virtuous as we can.

If you consistently remind yourself that you are mortal, that you won't live forever, you will create a mindset that will help you choose your actions more wisely. Being aware of your mortality will also prevent you from feeling sad about death. Instead, you will start enjoying your life even more. You will start appreciating the little things more; nothing will ever again be taken for granted.

Contemplating your mortality will help you stop paying attention to insignificant things. You will be able to focus on the important aspects of your life. You will stop making random choices, losing control to your emotions. You will become more rational and able to make choices for the greater good of your loved ones and the society you live in.

Keep *Memento Mori* in front of your eyes. You can write it down and place it on an easily visible stand. Or use an artistic symbol that will represent this idiom. Keep yourself aware of the passing of everything. It will make you appreciate your life more, the lives of everyone else, and also the beauty of nature. It can be part of your morning ritual, glance at the scripture *Memento Mori*, and remember each morning how lucky you are to be alive at this exact time. Remember all things pass and savor each and every moment of the life you have now.

Keeping a Journal

Just like Marcus Aurelius with his *Meditations*, or Seneca with his *Letters*, you want to write down your daily observations. Plans, reflections, thoughts, and observations should be written down in a journal from which you will later be able to read. You can read to yourself or for others, and this will encourage you to develop further, discuss your thoughts, and improve your observations. This is another practice you can do alone, and wherever you are, provided you have the means to write. It doesn't even have to be a notebook like in the old days. There are various apps today that will help you run your digital journal from your phone or computer. We live in an age where you won't have to wait until you get home to write down your thoughts. Wherever you are, if you feel the need, just write it down, and later you can reflect on it.

Journaling is a very useful activity, even if it serves the purpose of just letting your thoughts out. Psychiatrists and therapists often use this method in the treatment of their patients, as the simple act of writing down our thoughts helps us understand them better. There's something very powerful about putting our ideas and observations into words, it brings a realization that might elude us if we keep the thought only in our heads.

Epictetus used to tell his students to write down some philosophy every day. Writing helps people express themselves. Seneca was another big advocate of writing his philosophical observations. He said that doing so in the evening, when his mind was free to reflect on his day, helped him hide nothing from himself and judge his actions with logic. He said this even helped him sleep as he will have no stray thoughts or feelings left to disturb him. Of all the ancient Stoics, Marcus Aurelius was the most prodigious in journaling. Although he never intended for his private journal to be published, we are lucky it survived through the ages and his wisdom is still available to us.

In Stoicism, the art of journaling is so much more than simply writing down your thoughts to express them and to give them meaning. It is more than "dear diary..." It is philosophy. The journal is part of the Stoic philosopher; it is his way of life. It is the thoughts, reflections, plans, exercises, lessons learned, and lessons to pass on. A Stoic never finishes his journal and keeps this practice throughout his life. It is the way to rationality, virtue, and best version of himself. The journal is his means for a life-well-lived.

Today, you can even buy Stoic journals that are designed to help you write down your reflections and thoughts. They are the merge of Marcus' morning reflections and Seneca's evening "cases to his own court." They already contain some premises that will push you into thinking about important Stoic observations. But it is not necessary to buy one of these journals. You can create your own and design it in such a way that helps you get the most out of it. Give it a chance and discover its potential to turn you into the best version of yourself. You might be surprised how well a journal works on the human psyche. To get inspired, try reading "Meditations" by Marcus Aurelius, or the "Letters" by Seneca.

Practicing Discomfort

Remember the practice where you were compelled to foresee the bad? This one will take you one step further and ask you to practice the bad. The Stoics of old practiced living in discomfort, as through practice, they gained insight on how to deal with it and how to conquer it. In order to ensure your best response to future uncomfortable situations, why not practice some discomfort now? The goal of this form of training won't be to put a stone inside your shoe for the sake of feeling discomfort in and of itself. The purpose is to understand how true it is that material comfort doesn't correlate with happiness. You will start appreciating more what you do have, and you will be prepared to deal with the unpredictable and uncomfortable situations of life.

These exercises can be as challenging as you want to make them. But once you practice enough, you will start being just fine with what you now see as discomfort. Remember, this has to be voluntary, and you should practice it only if you want to. Nonetheless, they are not really as hard as they sound. They are not life-threatening discomforts, and keep in mind that you should never take it to the extremes. There are three basic discomfort situations you could put yourself into in order to practice.

Temporary poverty:

Dedicate a few days a month to live as less fortunate than you already are. This doesn't mean you need to be rich to practice living like a poor person. Just lower your standards slightly and be creative. Eat the cheapest food for a week, get rid of some of your fancy clothes and dress simpler. Try fasting for a day, sleeping on the floor, or simply tightening your monthly budget. Avoid restaurants or delivery food for a month. Try spending the night outside, sleeping in the open. There are many things you can do to practice enduring poverty.

I'll give you an example: A couple of months ago, I was going through a difficult situation in my personal life. I knew I needed to clear my head. So, one night, I decided to sleep in the garden. It was a really cold winter night. On purpose, I left all doors locked and went to sleep outside without any keys, so there was no turning back. I had to endure the night. I was "trapped" in my own garden with no smartphone, no technology at all, no food, no water, anything but a pack of cigarettes that I found in my jacket. Despite the cold, the rain, and the discomfort of sleeping on the hard, dirty floor without a pillow; it ended up being a great experience. I had all night to clear my thoughts, reflect, and actually slept well.

Put yourself in uncomfortable situations:

Again, you don't have to do this every day. You could

dedicate one day a month to put yourself into an extremely uncomfortable situation. It can be anything really, and once again, you get to be creative. You can decide not to use an umbrella during the rainy or snowy day. You can wear a silly hat or dress, so that everyone laughs at you; this way you practice against fear of criticism. Walk, imagine your car is broken and you have to walk the distance, or even use public transportation. Take a cold shower from time to time, just to feel the discomfort.

This is one of my favorite ones; every morning when I wake-up, I go right-ahead to take my cold (freezing) morning shower. This prepares my mind and body to face the day ahead. It gives me a feeling of victory, first thing in the morning, over my lazy, pleasure-seeking self, and I feel ready to conquer the day.

The purpose of these exercises is to toughen you up, to strengthen your character. Conquer fear of poverty, fear of criticism, and any other fear that enslaves you.

Avoid pleasure on purpose:

This one sounds so simple, but once you come into a situation to pass on something that will bring you instant pleasure, you will realize how much self-discipline and restraint you need.

Pass on an offered piece of cake, don't watch that movie you really wanted to, don't go to a party no matter how awesome it sounds. With this practice, you are not trying to completely deprive yourself of pleasures, but to train yourself in temperance. You do not have to do this every day, you decide how often you want to practice.

Remember that these exercises are not about punishing yourself but about training yourself for future discomforts. Your self-discipline, confidence, and resilience will certainly increase if you continue practicing intentional discomfort. And remember, you do not have to resign from the comfortable life completely. Determine how often you should practice the discomfort as only you can set the boundaries for yourself.

> "Set aside a certain number of days, during which you shall be content with the scantiest and cheapest fare, with coarse and rough

dress, saying to yourself the while: Is this the condition that I feared?

It is precisely in times of immunity from care that the soul should toughen itself beforehand for occasions of greater stress, and it is while Fortune is kind that it should fortify itself against her violence."

— SENECA, *LETTER XVIII*

V. WHEN THINGS GET TOUGH

In this part of the book, you will discover another set of principles and practices you can perform in order to train yourself as a Stoic. We will divide these practices in two groups. The first group will consist of practices for *challenging life situations*. You will learn how to act in accordance with nature, using reason to handle these situations in the best possible light. The second group of practices are for *situations with others*. They will help you deal with different aspects of human relationships, especially with difficult people.

When things get tough in life, Stoic principles can help you get out of the dark situation. During hard times the true Stoic will be recognized. When life becomes an uphill battle, we tend to forget about our principles. We normally lose our calm and rationality. It is important then, to learn how to deal with negative situations with virtue and reason. Life is not an easy ride, and you will get punched and kicked occasionally. The key is to learn how to respond to those punches and kicks with sound reason. To not give in to emotional responses, which will result in nothing beneficial.

You have to be aware that at some point in your life you will lose a loved one, you will get sick, or face other critical conditions. There will be times when it'll seem that everything is against you. That's life. We all face difficult times, but it is in our power to deal with them effectively and to rise above whatever life throws at us. In Marcus Aurelius' words: "Nothing happens to anybody which he is not fitted by nature to bear."

Dealing with Grief

When we lose someone we love, grief is the feeling that surrounds us. If we are not careful in our grief, we might allow it to suffocate us and crush us. Grief can be paralyzing, and you may find yourself unable to keep going on. Prolonged grief even leads to types of clinical depression, which would demand serious treatment.

As a Stoic, it is natural to feel the loss of your loved one. We are not deprived of emotions, nor do we suppress them. But, we are capable of recognizing, acknowledging, and dealing with those feelings. We do not hide from the emotions; we face them. Nonetheless, grief is only natural to some extent.

The grief you feel shows that you are an affectionate man or a woman; you did love the person that just passed away. However, if you feel that grief is of outmost importance, and it starts leading you to self-pity, you are about to cross the boundary of natural grief. Anything over this natural boundary can be considered vanity.

You might ask how grief can come off as vanity? It is because if you are grieving for too long, you are doing it for selfish reasons. This means you are grieving the good times you will never again have with your loved one instead of grieving the person. If you give in, your grief will show to be more about you and less about the loved one, and that is vanity.

This doesn't mean you shouldn't cry; of course, you are going to cry and feel sorrow when you lose a loved one. But you know that at some point you have to stop crying. Tears will not flow forever, and you must learn that it is appropriate to let go. After a natural period of time, crying and grieving will do you more harm than good. As a Stoic, you should always strive to have a good life; therefore, excessive grief is pointless.

There are things you could do to end your grief at a more appropriate time. Try thinking how worse you would be without ever having the chance to meet the person who just passed away. Go back to your journal and your *Memento Mori* contemplation and find comfort in the realization that everything needs to pass. Be grateful for all the special moments and experiences you had with them. Let reason lead you away from the grief because there is no point in it. Life does go on, and the universe is not against you. It is our nature to pass away.

Grief is somewhat contagious, and if others are grieving, we can "catch" it. If a friend is grieving for someone, we should be respectful and empathize to some extent, but we should not grieve with that person. Be there for your friend, but do not allow his grief to overwhelm you. Out of respect, it is appropriate to display the outward signs of grief, but do not give in to it. After all, our goal when someone else is grieving is to help them overcome the death of their loved one. If we join that person in grief, we are doing more harm both to our friend and to ourselves. What you can do for the grieving person is to let them know you understand them, support them, and be there to give a helping hand.

Dealing with Anger

What is anger? Seneca says it is an irrational desire to repay suffering. It is brief madness. Anger is a passion, a negative emotion that has to be tamed. An angry man is quick to forget kinship and lose reason, as he cannot discern between true and false. An angry person does not have self-control. Letting anger take over brings nothing positive to your life; it can only hurt you. The damage caused by anger can be catastrophic and irreversible. Think about how many people in a moment of outrage, end up harming their loved ones with words or deeds.

Once anger takes over, it is really hard to go back to reason. Anger is madness, and we cannot lose control to it. For Stoics, the key to mastering anger is to control our initial reactions. Most often, we find ourselves unable to control that first reaction. Nonetheless, we do have the capacity to reject such initial reactions and continue acting with reason. Anger is giving in to our emotions, but as rational beings, we should be able to do much better than that.

Some people argue that anger helps them be brave, and that there are some things they wouldn't achieve without being driven by anger. However, anger does not help courage; it takes its place. A person who cannot be brave without anger is not brave at all. What's courageous is taking rational action, being fully aware of what the consequences might be. Anger should never be the force that drives us. We can find that force in love, compassion, and justice. Anger is unpredictable and dangerous. Why should we allow ourselves to lose control of our temper? We should be compelled to act courageously by our values and principles. Only in this manner we can be certain we are doing the right thing.

In the end, anger is a choice. You can choose not to be a madman. Never respond to anger with anger. If someone you're dealing with suddenly becomes an angry beast, as a Stoic, you remain calm and sober. Even if you're facing an opponent, your best-bet is always to keep a clear-head. Your duty is to not become like the wrongdoer, but to act as the rational being that you are. Through reason, you can show the angered person a better path. After all, it is not external events what cause our suffering, but our own opinions about them. You can show the angered person how to see things in a different perspective.

Dealing with Fear

Fear holds us back, paralyzes us, and do not allows us to act rationally. There are different forms of fear, and although sometimes fear might be helpful by warning us of dangers ahead, most of our fears are normally irrational. The damage of the object of our fear is often negligible compared to the damage the fear itself can cause, especially if we are blinded by it. No matter if the fear is grounded or ungrounded, we must always keep a clear-head if we want to get ourselves out of dangerous situations.

An ungrounded fear is when we project the negative outcome of a possible future event. Let's say, you are overwhelmed by anxiety and fear of a crucial meeting with your boss, which is to be held ten days from now. In this case, the cause of the fear is an external event which you do not have control of. What you can control is your emotions and your response to the situation. Prepare yourself to the best of your ability to that meeting, and let the chips fall where they may. When you know you've done your best, fear goes away, and you realize there was nothing to be afraid of in the first place. For the Stoics, as you may remember, the opposite to fear is called *Caution*.

A grounded fear is when you encounter an actual threat to your existence and well-being. For example, facing someone in the street who is trying to harm you. Even though the threat is real, you can't allow fear to take over. A man may hurt you more easily if he can see your weakness. Therefore, you must keep a clear-head and think rationally about how to get yourself out of this situation. Even the simple act of running away, if possible, may be a rational solution. The best you can do is to keep control of your emotions and actions, and not let fear paralyze you. It's always a better stay rational and confront the situation you are in with caution and courage.

Another form of fear is the fear of loss. We tend to

attach ourselves to objects or people, and we are afraid of losing them. We've already learned that nothing is eternal; everything must pass. Even our own death will tear us apart of everything we are attached to. The fact that everything is transitory is evident. This is why we must detach ourselves from all objects and outcomes that are out of our control. It is precisely this lack of control that leads to fear. It is not to very difficult to understand the reasons why we must be emotionally detached from our material possessions. But what about people? Must we not attach ourselves to anyone?

We are social beings, and we do need other people as they need us. It's only natural to have different kinds of relationships with our family, friends, and partners. But, how do we avoid the fear of losing the people we love? The answer may be in anticipation. The time will come when we're going to lose a loved one. If we are well-prepared, we will have no fear. If you anticipate losses, once they come, you won't be easily devastated. And do not forget, anticipating calamities is not about being pessimistic and ruining the present. It is the most rational way to deal with whatever the future may bring.

Phobias are another great example of irrational

fears. Of course, we are not talking about pathological phobias that need attention from professionals, but the little irrational fears that we all have. Take, for example, the fear of spiders. Most people who are afraid of spiders have never even touched one in their life. They don't have any kind of experience with the arachnids, except they are aware of their existence. So, what exactly are they afraid of? Especially when it is the spider who should be afraid of them, as they pose more danger to its existence.

Phobias are like nightmares, once you wake up, you realize there was nothing to be afraid of in the first place. They are not real. They are irrational. But spiders are very much real. Yes, they are, but the danger they pose to your existence is minimal. This is why your fear is irrational, and you must use reason to confront it.

In the end, it is not wise to hide our fears, pretend they do not exist, and become reckless. Fear is our automatic response to the dangers of our existence. Fear may be helpful when it warns us of real threats. However, we must confront it, rationalize it, and turn it into action. We must stop attaching ourselves to the things that are out of our control, and we have to use reason to analyze our fears in order to act upon them. Little by little, we can free ourselves from the negative aspects of fear.

Dealing with Pain and Provocation

Stoics often say, "what stands in the way becomes the way." We can use the obstacle to our advantage. We must understand that when we are in physical pain, it is only our body that is in pain. Our mind can still function, and it needs to function clearly. When in pain, we can even practice our virtues, such as patience, endurance, and willpower. It is the same with disease. Your body is ill, not your mind. Of course, we are not talking about life-threatening diseases that may have an impact on the human mind, but about small diseases like the common flu.

Look at the example of Epictetus, who we already know was lame. He did not let his lameness stop him; he understood that it was his leg that was sick, not his mind. When we are in pain or sickness, we often resort to self-pity. A Stoic must not allow self-pity to overcome him because it will only increase the suffering, and nothing good will come out of it. A Stoic must remember that pain is the opportunity to practice and test his virtue.

There is no need to actively seek pain and suffering in order to practice your virtues, the opportunities will arise, and they will be various. Pain is just one of the opportunities, and if you keep your mind clear and unaffected by pain, it will be much easier for you to realize the potential of your inner strength. But pain is not only physical; sometimes, people can cause us pain with their actions or words. We call those actions provocations as they are designed to extort an emotional reaction from us. They are a perfect opportunity for a Stoic to display his virtues.

If someone insults you, for example, use your rational mind. You will realize there is no point in returning the insult. Instead, try practicing patience, stay cool, and let your opponent say whatever he wants. Even if he is saying hurtful things, you, as a Stoic, must remain calm and let it pass. Once your opponent is done, confront him with reason and with fact. There is no dignity in responding to the insults with violence. Be the best version of yourself, choose to abide by reason, and be the first to walk away from fruitless arguments.

Overcoming Challenges

Life is never easy or fair. Nevertheless, through kicks and punches that life throws at us, we grow and improve ourselves. We learn how to endure and survive, we keep building our character with different experiences, and we mature in the process. The absence of challenges leads to stagnation. We cannot exercise virtue if we do not encounter obstacles. Take a look at the old Greek myth about Hercules, the hero. Would he ever be considered a hero if he had no obstacles to conquer? If life didn't throw challenges his way? Where would Hercules be without the lion, the Hydra, and the apples of the Hesperides? If you are unfamiliar with the myth of Hercules, I encourage you to read about his twelve labors. They are a great allegory for obstacles we all encounter during our lives, and the character we need to have to overcome them all.

It is the challenges in lives that shape us into what we are to become. We cannot control these challenges as they are external events. However, yet again, we can control our own actions responding to those challenges. It is our actions that will determine what kind of person we'll become. Will you allow yourself to become a weak and cowardly person, or will you control your actions and live to fulfill your highest potential? Only if we act with virtue in spite of life's challenges, will we ever reach the best version of ourselves.

You do not have to go out and actively seek these challenges. Every person will face their fair share of them by simply being alive. However, when the challenges do come, do not fall into self-pity and take the victim role. Instead, gather strength, wisdom, courage, and face the challenges. When we face adversity, and respond to it to the best of our ability, we learn a lot about ourselves. How will you know what your capacities are if you never face any challenge? You will continue through life without ever realizing your potential.

Stoics engage actively in life in order to meet the challenges. They do not close themselves up in the ivory towers and wait for the events to pass them by. They constantly grow and work on themselves to become better people and to contribute to the society they live in. This is why the next time you have a difficult challenge in front of you, embrace the opportunity it gives you to improve yourself. For sure, life will throw some punches at you, and the only question is when. So, be prepared, anticipate misfortunes, and learn from the experience they provide.

When we are talking about the challenges life can present us with, we often think about the unfortunate events that may happen that we cannot prevent at all. However, we often forget that most of our day-to-day troubles come from our relationship with other people. Very often you will meet with annoying or toxic people that may compel you into irrational behavior. It can even be someone who you don't even care for, an accidental encounter on the street, a driver who cut you off, a nagging nurse at the hospital, or even the annoying little girl screaming for attention.

You would think it is easy to get rid of these people, so many new philosophies tell you to just push them out of your life or pretend they don't exist. However, should you really do it? Some of those negative people may be your loved ones. You are not supposed to get rid of them. As a human being, you have a deep, natural connection with other people. Imagine if you just keep pushing everyone away from your life. You will end up lonely, and what happens to a human who is alone? They wither away.

Above all, we have a social duty towards our community. As a Stoic, you have to help others and contribute to the well-being of humankind. Stoicism proposes that we are all citizens of the world, and that we ought to treat each other as relatives. After all, we are individuals of the same nature. We cannot exist without other people, and we all have our roles in to play in society.

People's Motivations

Nobody is doing something wrong on purpose unless there is a pathological side to it. Even then, we cannot say it's completely willingly as we don't know what may prevent a person from thinking and acting rationally. This is why we should never blame people for their wrongdoings, even when they're turned towards us. When people are rude or unfair, there is always a reason for it, and instead of lashing out in response, we should try to understand what is going on.

Stoicism teaches us that people always act how they think it's the best way to act. However, this does not mean that all people act rationally. They are not aware that in the long-term, lying is not going to benefit their cause; stealing is not going to bring them wealth. It is the lack of reason that drives people to make wrong decisions. Why do they lack reason? Because they do not live in accordance with nature. They do not pay attention to facts, and they do not possess the wisdom that will allow them to act with virtue. Their own emotions possess them, and instead of trying to control them, they often let them take control, and all they do is blindly follow.

Because people do not do wrong with purpose, or they do it with false purpose, we must understand them and show patience. After all, we do not know everything that led those people to do wrong. We cannot know their background, how they grew up, what their habits are, or what is in their psyche. Maybe they were less fortunate than we are, their DNA is different, or simply they do not possess enough wisdom. Whatever the reasons, a Stoic must be aware he does not have all the information he needs in order to pass judgment. Instead of judging, we can remain calm, patient, and understanding. Remind yourself that you are privileged and that your opponent might have had a bad childhood, insufficient education, or was exposed to violence.

There is no reason for feeling anger or resentment towards these people. What a Stoic has to do when encountering such a person, is to lead by example.

Be the one who will pass the reason, not judgment. You must be the beacon of virtue and show the right path. When other people act wrongly is an opportunity for you and for them to grow and develop. Lead by example if you want others to behave in a virtuous and rational manner.

The Faults Within You

Now that you understand that there may be a variety of unknown causes that drive people to do wrong; ask yourself, are you in the same boat with them? Nobody is perfect, and we all make mistakes, but we tend to forget our own and put the blame only on others. Nobody does wrong on purpose, and this is true for you as well. Look into your past and remember a time when you did something wrong. Analyze the events that led you to that wrongdoing, what was the force that drove you? Most often, it is either emotion or ignorance.

Stoics are not perfect, and we all make mistakes. What we can always do is to strive to embody our highest ideals. It is not perfection that matters, but the path to it. Even though you will never achieve perfection, you will live a good life filled with virtue as you give your best to fulfill your highest potential. However, to be able to start the journey towards becoming a Stoic sage, a wise man, you must recognize your own faults and learn how to deal with them. You might be quick to anger, or you might cling on desires. No matter what it may be, you need to recognize it as a fault and try to get rid of it.

If you gain insight into your own faults, you will be able to understand other people better and why they are failing or doing wrong. The same emotion that drove you to yell at your loved one might be why someone else yelled at you. Our brains tend to rationalize our failings and come up with an excuse for it. Do not accept excuses; there are none. Don't let your mind trick you into believing that your wrongdoings are justified because you had good intentions. You might as well accept other people's wrong behavior in the same way. There is no excuse for the wrong. The Stoic should always strive to do what is right and what is true. It is the only way to contribute to humanity and to live a fulfilling life.

Acting with Kindness

There is a nice African proverb that says, "kindness

is a language which the blind can see, and the deaf can hear." The meaning of this proverb is that if you show kindness to people who are driven by emotions and are giving in to passions, you can change them, and they will understand their faults. If you encounter an angry friend, and he lashes out at you, instead of responding to anger with anger, show kindness. It may be that your friend will see the kindness and accept it, as if you used a magic word. He would probably understand his behavior is irrational, and apologize for lashing at you.

Kindness is truly magical. You probably have experienced it either as a recipient or as a giver. People tend to reward kindness with kindness. Help the old lady cross the street, and she might give you candy. Help the new neighbor move in, and you might get invited to dinner. Encountering people is always an opportunity to practice kindness. And it doesn't even have to be with people. You can even show kindness to animals. Feed the stray dog, and you will get a friend for life. Of course, you should never be kind expecting the reward. Kindness in itself is of great value.

Stoics believe we were born with kindness, and it is in our nature to express it. Kindness works, and it improves ours and other people's lives. As our goal is a fulfilling life, kindness is a virtue we must possess. There is strength in kindness, and can practice it every day. It's enough to smile at your neighbors, or start small talk showing care for people's well-being. Be thankful when other people show kindness in return. There is love in kindness.

> "Hecato says, 'I can teach you a love potion made without any drugs, herbs, or special spell— if you would be loved, love."
>
> — SENECA, *LETTER IX*

VI. TIMELESS WISDOM

We all sometimes need a little inspiration, a little nudge forward to spark the thinking process. Thinking and observing are the main tools of Stoics, as they are so natural to humans. They are the force that will keep us going, especially when we feel stuck. They will enlighten us and show us the way. Although Stoics acknowledge epiphany (a moment of sudden realization), we cannot rely on it, we cannot just wait for a big breakthrough. Instead, Stoics prefer to rely on their ability to think, observe, and draw conclusions in a consistent basis. It is an ongoing process as events keep happening, we keep meeting new people, and finding ourselves in new situations.

Everything deserves our attention, and everything can bring realization.

When getting started on this path, we might not be able to think clearly and draw the right conclusions as we are still influenced by our emotions. What matters is that you keep striving to improve yourself. When this happens, it is important to have an inspiration that will help you come to the right conclusions. And who are better for the task than the Stoics of Old, the ones who started it all and the ones whose thoughts keep inspiring us in the modern age. Let's take a look at their writings, the thoughts they shared with us, and see how they can help in our personal quest for wisdom. You've been already introduced to some of them in the first chapter and learned their story. Let's now take a look at their work, their thoughts and observations.

Seneca

Seneca was a fascinating philosopher. His life as a Roman noble is worth our attention with all the richness and intrigue the status brought him. I highly recommend that you read about Seneca's life as well. He was a man with a turbulent life and only one constant that kept him centered throughout everything that happened in his life - philosophy. However, Seneca often borrowed ideas from other schools to develop his own perspective on Stoicism and improve his character. His early teacher in philosophy was Attalus, a man who Seneca often quotes and speaks highly about. In his writings, he often mentions Cato, who was a senator, eloquent orator, and a philosopher who had a great influence on young Seneca. Of the non-Stoic philosophers, Seneca was most greatly influenced by Epicurus, who he mentions with great respect.

Since Seneca draws inspiration from his teachers and other philosophers of his time, or even before, we should allow ourselves to be influenced by Seneca. Renowned people throughout history, from different walks of life, such as Erasmus, Francis Bacon, Pascal, and Montaigne talked about their admiration for Seneca. There is a great revival of interest for Seneca's work in modern days, and plenty of books talk about his life and his philosophy. However, do not forget that Seneca's work lives today in the form his most famous book titled *Letters from a Stoic*. In some cases, you might find it titled *Moral Letters to Lucilius* or *Moral Epistles*. Seneca was a master in the practical part of philosophy, and probably this is why he is still relevant today.

In the first of Seneca's thoughts, we will observe, he urges his friend Lucilius to find a role model. This role model will serve him as an anchor and provide him with the standard to live by. Of course, this idea is not new to Stoicism or humanity; however, Seneca puts it in a perspective from which we can see why having a role model is necessary in our pursuit of the good life.

> "So choose yourself a Cato—or, if Cato seems too severe for you, a Laelius, a man whose character is not quite so strict. Choose someone whose way of life as well as words, and whose very face as mirroring the character that lies behind it, have won your approval. Be always pointing him out to yourself either as your guardian or as your model. There is a need, in my view, for someone as a standard against which our characters can measure themselves. Without a ruler to do it against, you won't make crooked straight."

Seneca was a somewhat paradoxical person. He was a very wealthy man who claimed he did not cared about wealth. It may be because he did not develop a dependency on his wealth. He did not succumb to the extravagance, passions, and depravity of the wealthy and powerful of the time. He was the master, not a slave. As Seneca teaches us, we constantly need to remind ourselves that material possessions are indifferent, and we shouldn't allow ourselves to get trapped in fear of losing our wealth. As he wrote in *On the Happy Life*:

> "For the wise man does not consider himself unworthy of any gifts from Fortune's hands: he does not love wealth, but he would rather have it; he does not admit into his heart but into his home; and what wealth is his he does not reject but keeps, wishing it to supply greater scope for him to practice his virtue. For the wise man regards wealth as a slave, the fool as a master."

Some other thoughts by Seneca you might find useful in your pursuit of wisdom:

"No person has the power to have everything they want, but it is in their power not to want what they don't have, and to cheerfully put to good use what they do have."

"True happiness is to enjoy the present, without anxious dependence upon the future, not to amuse ourselves with either hopes or fears but to rest satisfied with what we have, which is sufficient, for he that is so wants nothing. The greatest blessings of mankind are within us and within our reach. A wise man is content with his lot, whatever it may be, without wishing for what he has not."

"Life is like a play: it's not the length, but the excellence of the acting that matters."

Marcus Aurelius

As a Roman Emperor, he held the whole power of the Western World in his hands. A warrior, a ruler, and a Stoic, Marcus Aurelius was a true practitioner of philosophy. He was in a position where it was easy to indulge in vice and temptation without anyone protesting. There was no one who could put a restraint on him. Yet he did put it on himself. He did not want to become a corrupted ruler, and he did everything he could for his Roman people. He is known as the last of the *Five Good Emperors of Rome*.

He was a true beacon of wisdom and virtue, and he ruled by them. As a Stoic figure of humanity's history, Marcus Aurelius is still regarded as one of the best rulers the world has ever known. Marcus was a very practical philosopher, and, as we've mentioned, he left behind his private diary now published under the title *Meditations*. He never intended to have an audience; he wrote for himself to be able to remember his thoughts and observations, to remind himself of the way to the good life.

For Emperor Marcus Aurelius, philosophy was the way to escape the temptations of his position. He used it to deal with daily complex situations as the leader of a great empire would certainly encounter. His Stoic philosophy concentrated on social duty, self-restraint, and respect towards others. The virtues his successors managed to forget in their times of rule.

Marcus Aurelius also teaches us how not to drown

in self-pity and jealousy when we lack certain talents that come naturally to others. If you catch yourself thinking, why aren't you good at one thing, ask yourself what are you good at and focus on improving the virtues that you possess.

"No one could ever accuse you of being quick-witted. All right, but there are plenty of other things you can't claim you 'haven't got in you.' Practice the virtues you can show: honesty, gravity, endurance, austerity, resignation, abstinence, patience, sincerity, moderation, seriousness, high-mindedness. Don't you see how much you have to offer—beyond excuses like 'can't?' And yet you still settle for less."

We all have moments when we feel down when we are defeated and think that there is no point in continuing with a certain task. As Seneca, Marcus Aurelius teaches us the importance of role models. They can help us with encouragement, strength, and duty.

> "When you need encouragement, think of the qualities the people around you have: this one's energy, that one's modesty, another's generosity, and so on. Nothing is as encouraging as when virtues are visibly embodied in the people around us when we're practically showered with them. It's good to keep this in mind."

Remember the exercise where you need to practice *negative visualization*? Marcus Aurelius was aware of the benefits of such a practice; however, he noticed that it might have an unwanted side effect. A crippling fear might envelop us if we dwell too much on possible negative outcomes. To fight that side effect, Marcus wrote:

> "Don't let your imagination be crushed by life as a whole. Don't try to picture everything bad that could possibly happen. Stick with the situation at hand, and ask, "Why is this so unbearable? Why can't I endure it?" You'll be embarrassed to answer. Then remind yourself that the past and future have no

power over you. Only the present—and even that can be minimized. Just mark off its limits. And if your mind tries to claim that it can't hold out against that…well, then, heap shame upon it."

Here are some of my favorite notes that Marcus Aurelius wrote down as thoughts and observations:

"Yes, you can–if you do everything as if it were the last thing you were doing in your life, and stop being aimless, stop letting your emotions override what your mind tells you, stop being hypocritical, self-centered, irritable."

"At dawn, when you have trouble getting out of bed, tell yourself: 'I have to go to work – as a human being. What do I have to complain of, if I'm going to do what I was born for – the things I was brought into the world to do? Or is this what I was created for? To huddle under the blankets and stay warm?'"

"When you wake up in the morning, tell yourself: The people I deal with today will be meddling, ungrateful, arrogant, dishonest, jealous, and surely. They are like this because they can't tell good from evil."

"The best way of avenging thyself is not to become like the wrong-doer"

"No carelessness in your actions. No confusion in your words. No imprecision in your thoughts."

Epictetus

The beauty of Stoicism is that it touches all levels of society. We had a Roman noble in Seneca, an Emperor in Marcus Aurelius, and now we have Epictetus, who was a slave. It is amazing that no matter what your background might be, Stoicism is always the same. It provides us with the principles that can cross time and social stature and apply to all aspects of our lives. We are all entitled to the good life, we can all work on the things in our power to achieve it.

We can only imagine what hardships Epictetus endured during his life as a slave, but we know his Stoic philosophy had an influence on many people, among them Emperor Marcus Aurelius. The strength of the slave's words was such that it moved even an Emperor. Nowadays, Epictetus continues to inspire many people. James Stockdale a Prisoner of War for seven years during the Vietnamese War, says he turned to Epictetus to gather the strength for the torture he was put through. It was Epictetus who said:

> "Sickness is a hindrance to the body, but not to your ability to choose unless that is your choice. Lameness is a hindrance to the leg,

but not to your ability to choose. Say this to yourself with regard to everything that happens, then you will see such obstacles as hindrances to something else, but not to yourself."

To start reading Epictetus's work, maybe it would be best to devote some time to "Enchiridion." It is a small philosophy handbook packed with his thoughts and observations in the form of short maxims. It was written by his student Arrian as Epictetus himself never wrote anything.

The most well-known quote from Epictetus is about one of the main principles of Stoicism, and it teaches us that there are things we control and things we do not have control of. He makes a clear difference between these two by saying:

"Some things are in our control and others not. Things in our control are opinion, pursuit, desire, aversion, and, in a word, whatever are our own actions. Things not in our control are body, property, reputation,

> command, and, in a word, whatever are not our own actions."

Knowing how his students' minds tend to wander during his teachings, Epictetus talked about the importance of character. He tasked his students with setting some principles and standards they will stick to and not deviate from them. It is a difficult task to put on anyone, but significant for Stoics as it will give them clear direction to follow and bring them closer to the character they want to have.

> "Immediately prescribe some character and form of conduct to yourself, which you may keep both alone and in company."

Some other very interesting ideas from Epictetus:

"If someone tried to take control of your body and make you a slave, you would fight for freedom. Yet how easily you hand over your mind to anyone who insults you. When you dwell on their words and let them dominate your thoughts, you make them your master."

"Happiness and freedom begin with a clear understanding of one principle. Some things are under your control, and some things are not"

"If anyone tells you that a certain person speaks ill of you, do not make excuses about what is said of you but answer, "He was ignorant of my other faults, else he would not have mentioned these alone."

"Demand not that events should happen as you wish, but wish them to happen as they do happen, and your life will be serene."

Cleanthes

A student of the father of Stoicism, Zeno, Cleanthes, had a dual life. A philosopher by day and water carrier by night, Cleanthes had to work during the night to support his daily pursuits for wisdom. He became the head of the Stoic school and held that position for 32 years. He died at the age of 99; however, very little of his writings survived to the modern age. In fact, his only surviving work is his hymn to Zeus. However, through the work of Diogenes Laertius and his *"Lives of the Eminent Philosophers,"* which I fully recommend reading, we can learn about some of the things Cleanthes pondered.

On human ability to think and reason and how it separates us from animals, Cleanthes wrote:

> "Ignorant men differ from beasts only in their figure."

Cleanthes also believed in fate, and his teachings were about following it. However, the fate for Stoics is all the events and things that are beyond our control. Instead of fighting what we cannot control, we must follow the events and see where they will lead us. Some other quotes by Cleanthes that concern fate:

"The willing are led by fate, the reluctant are dragged."

"The Fates guide the person who accepts them and hinder the person who resists them."

Cato

A soldier, an aristocrat, a senator, and a Stoic, Cato is a well-known figure in Roman history as the last man standing when the Republic fell. He was an enemy of Julius Caesar who fought to the last breath for liberty. To the Founding Fathers of America, Cato was a symbol of liberty, and they often quoted him. Washington, John Adams, Benjamin Franklin, all knew Cato's work very well and admired his principles. When Patrick Henry asked King George to grant him liberty or death, he was quoting Cato. Nathan Hale borrowed from Cato when he said he regrets having only one life to give for his country.

Even though today we remember Caesar, but barely anyone remembers Cato, he was a worthy opponent. He was Caesar's equal in eloquence, duty, and force of character. He was a politician, capable of giving a moving speech in front of the Senate. It was his political defeat that cost him his place in history, as we all know it, history is written by the victors.

He also didn't leave anything in written form behind him. He never wrote about his military successes, as Caesar did. He never rose monuments to himself. As in life, so in his philosophy, he was all about living it, not writing it. The only surviving writing we have from Cato is one short letter. It is through the work of Greek biographer Plutarch that we know of the life of Cato the Younger and his philosophical ideas. To learn more about Cato, I recommend that you read any prominent biographers' work on Cato, as they are all based on Plutarch's work and the works of contemporary writers such as Cicero or Thrasea Paetus who was a fellow Stoic.

We do not have any quotes of Cato surviving to this day that we can use as maxims for thinking and observation; however, Cato's whole life is an inspiration for a Stoic. There are amazing modern works that concentrate on Cato, such as *Rome's Last Citizen:*

VI. TIMELESS WISDOM | 125

The Life and Legacy of Cato, Mortal Enemy of Caesar, by Jimmy Soni and Rob Goodman.

There are words prescribed to Cato through the pen of his biographers, and you can use them as a starting point to learn more about his life.

"I will begin to speak when I have that to say which had not better be unsaid."

"Bitter are the roots of study, but how sweet their fruit."

"An honest man is seldom a vagrant."

"In doing nothing, men learn to do evil."

"Consider in silence whatever anyone says:

speech both conceals and reveals the inner soul of man."

"Flee sloth, for the indolence of the soul, is the decay of the body."

The XXI Century Stoic

We live in a very chaotic world where time is of incredible significance, and we always seem to lack it. We are overstressed by work, school, relationships, and social lives in general. We do live in a new age where information is just one click away from us, and it can be a good thing. We gave voice to the marginalized groups of people, we can learn every minute of our days, and we have access to unlimited sources of information. These are all good things technology brought to us, but there is the other side of the coin.

We are also living in the age of anxiety; we care more about what others will think or say about us.

People were never before so distanced from each other yet dependent on others' opinions. As much as social networks enabled us to search for old friends and reconnect, they also pushed us away from people and the need for real-world contact. We keep ourselves at a distance, keeping most of our communications online in hopes it will hurt less if we are rejected or criticized. It is exactly here where Stoicism is needed and why, I think, the rediscovery of this ancient philosophy is on the rise.

The modern world keeps us in a constant state of reliance on external things, and we keep forgetting about the things we can control. People seek stress relief in things like gambling, porn, food, alcohol, and drugs. Short-lived pleasures that will make them feel good just for the moment. That moment is enough as long as they keep the problems outside of people's consciousness. There is no need to give a lecture on how these coping mechanisms are bad for an individual and for society. They lead to addiction and failure of humanity. We need to stop relying on these external mechanisms to escape our pain. They are no good in the long term, and they are downgrading our quality of life.

Instead, we should turn towards ourselves and see

what the inner world has to offer and how we can work on the things we have control over. Only if we work on ourselves and continue building our virtues, we will be able to be happy. Stoicism is a good path to achieve this because it is a philosophy that concentrates on the pragmatic side of life, while it also helps you build your inner world.

Even though Stoicism is an ancient philosophy, it is becoming more and more popular today because its advice is universal. Stoicism is relevant today because it deals with the issues that transcend time and space. It was applicable in the old Greek and Roman world, and we can still apply it today. It deals with problems that are above simple culture or politics. It deals with the human inside us.

Stoicism teaches us how to live as productive members of our community and as citizens of the world. It is a very pragmatic philosophy that teaches you how to behave in different situations. It gives you the strength to deal with misfortune, difficult people, sickness, and old age. Things that have always been a challenge for human beings. Stoicism is an answer to almost everyone's problems. It is a philosophy of the poor and the rich, for leaders and followers, for famous and unknown people.

Stoicism is a way of life, and it is an easy prescription for all the illnesses humans experience. However, as an individual, it requires hard work and training, as we are so easily distracted by the external world. One of the most difficult principles of Stoicism to acquire today must be self-discipline. It demands our full and undivided attention, something that is very difficult to keep up in the world where we are constantly being bombarded by external information. But we shouldn't give up just because it can be hard. In fact, it's the process that matters, not the end result. Just by trying to live by the Stoic principles, you may become a lot happier than ever before in your life.

Another good thing about modern Stoicism is that it gives people safe grounding needed in the times when we are uncertain of our environment. This grounding used to be provided by the community, the family, schools, churches. They are all less relevant in the modern age, and families break apart so easily. When everything is constantly shifting, changing, we need to have one constant in our lives that will always push us forward. Stoicism can be that constant, and it can provide us with certainty and safety. We know that philosophy can always safeguard our back, and nothing will be able to crush us anymore.

Stoicism is all about human nature. One of its main principles is "live in accordance with nature." It applied to the Classical philosophers in a different sense, but it is these principles that have stayed the same and relevant to this day. Maybe we do not believe in the divine nature of the universe anymore, but in the nature within us. Even though the perspective on nature slightly shifted in the modern world, it is the Stoic principles that still apply today. Virtue is still virtue, and we need to live with it in order to achieve happiness. It is the same happiness that people of old times were searching for. Human nature stayed the same, and our goals are still the same. It is with the same principles we will reach those goals.

There are plenty of old philosophies that are living again now in the modern age, such as Hedonism or Epicureanism, and just like the people of Classical times, you can pick the one that resonates more with you. In my opinion, Stoicism is superior for one simple reason. All of them rely on external things that are out of your control to make you happy. They propagate indulgence in vices or simpler pleasures, things which are not in our control. They are unreliable and unstable.

Stoicism, on the other hand, teaches you how to rely on yourself, how to build confidence, courage, and strength. If you are sure in yourself, there will be no external event that will be able to devastate you. You will be like a mountain, unmovable, and difficult to conquer. And just like the mountain, you will provide for the people, for the greater good of the community. There is no happiness in life without other people, as we are social beings. And this is another aspect where Stoicism will make a positive impact in your life.

In today's day and age, where people are distancing from each other, where people are extremely selfish and egocentric, it is on you, a Stoic, to reconnect with humans. Through your endeavor of giving and working for the community, you will be its active member. There will be no more hiding behind the social media for you; Stoicism will ask you to go out there and help the next person in need. You cannot practice your virtue if you do not face the challenges of everyday life as an active member of society.

Go out, help the neighbor or a stray dog, and see how Stoicism is shaping you into a better and stronger individual. Be the change you want to see in society and set an example for others to follow. And be sure people will follow, because kindness is always mirrored with kindness. People respond to goodness, and they will want to be happy themselves. Through your example of virtue, you will inspire others around you to act with virtue, and together you will create a better community.

As already mentioned so many times, Stoicism is to be practiced, not only studied. As a modern Stoic, you are expected to get out there and behave as a Stoic. But what does it all mean in the modern world? The differences between old and modern Stoicism are not that great, and what used to apply to Marcus Aurelius or Seneca applies to you too. Aim to always act with virtue.

Focus on the things you can control, such as your reason and behavior. Learn to live with others who aren't as wise as you. Also with those who are much wiser than you. Continue working on yourself and constantly improving. Set a goal of the perfect image of yourself and strive for it. Live each day with that image of perfection in front of your eyes. Remember that there is no external reward for virtue, only bonuses that may multiply throughout your life and make it easier.

No matter what your motivations are, what you are trying to achieve in your life, Stoicism is a foundation on which you can always build. Stoicism offers a framework for living a more harmonious and meaningful life, but it is on you to build that happiness, it does not come as a gift. Through constant work, there is a chance you will become a Stoic Sage, a wise man, maybe even by the measure of Zeno, Epictetus, or Seneca. No matter who you are now, it is who you can become that matters.

> "Be satisfied if you can live the rest of your life, however short, as your nature demands. Focus on that, and don't let anything distract you. You've wandered all over and finally realized that you never found what you were after: how to live. Not in syllogisms, not in money, or fame, or self-indulgence. Nowhere."
>
> — MARCUS AURELIUS,
> *MEDITATIONS*

THE 'STOICISM CLASSICS' - ULTIMATE BUNDLE

The *'Stoicism Classics'* collection includes:

1. The Meditations by Marcus Aurelius
2. The Discourses by Epictetus
3. Letters from a Stoic by Seneca

To get them for free, visit the following link:

www.unrivaledmind.com/classics

AFTERWORD

There are no mysterious secrets regarding Stoicism. It is a practical philosophy that focuses on bettering yourself, improving your life and the lives of those in your community. It is not religious belief, it does not involve any kind of faith in a higher power, and you don't need to perform any rituals.

We can summon up Stoicism with this premise: It makes no difference if you are rich or poor; beautiful or ugly; famous or unknown; healthy or sick; free or slave. All that is needed to lead a fulfilling life is virtue. Virtue is enough.

All you need to do is become a better human being. For your own benefit and the well-being of those around you. Study the ancient philosophers, live by their example, and strive to become the best version of yourself.

> "Very little is needed to make a happy life; it is all within yourself, in your way of thinking."
>
> — MARCUS AURELIUS

ONE LAST THING

Can I ask you a favor?

Could you leave a quick review of *An Introduction to Stoicism*?

I gladly read every single one of them.

To leave your review, go to the following link:

www.unrivaledmind.com/review

If you don't want to spend a lot of time, just write one sentence about what you enjoyed about the book.

I truly appreciate your feedback and support.

Thanks in advance,

Damian.

- "I'm a very simple man. All I need to be happy is reviews."

— DAMIAN ALEXANDER, 2020 A.D.

REFERENCES

Aurelius, M., Epictetus, Carus, T. L., Munro, H. A. J., Long, G., & Hutchins, R. M. (1952). *Great books of the western world, volume 12: Lucretius: on the nature of things; The discourses of Epictetus; The meditations of Marcus Aurelius*. Chicago: Encyclopedia Britannica, Inc.

Epictetus & Matheson, P. E. (1938). *Epictetus. The discourses and manual, together with fragments of his writings*. London: Oxford University Press.

Gerson, L. P. (2010). *The Cambridge history of philosophy in late Antiquity*. Cambridge: Cambridge University Press.

Sellars, J. (2006). *Stoicism*. Berkeley: University of California Press.

Strange, S. K., & Zupko, J. (2011). *Stoicism: traditions and transformations*. Cambridge: Cambridge University Press.

Made in the USA
Coppell, TX
01 July 2020